GREETING CARDS

in an afternoon™

GREETING CARDS
in an afternoon™

Cindy Gorder

Sterling Publishing Co., Inc.
New York

Prolific Impressions Production Staff:

Editor: Mickey Baskett
Copy: Phyllis Mueller
Graphics: Dianne Miller, Karen Turpin
Styling: Lenos Key
Photography: Jerry Mucklow
Administration: Jim Baskett

Library of Congress Cataloging-in-Publication Data Available

10 9 8 7 6 5 4 3 2

Published by Sterling Publishing Company, Inc.
387 Park Avenue South, New York, N.Y. 10016
Produced by Prolific Impressions, Inc.
160 South Candler St., Decatur, GA 30030
©2001 Prolific Impressions, Inc.
Distributed in Canada by Sterling Publishing
c/o Canadian Manda Group, One Atlantic Avenue, Suite 105
Toronto, Ontario, Canada M6K 3E7
Distributed in Great Britain and Europe by Cassell PLC
Wellington House, 125 Strand, London WC2R 0BB, England
Distributed in Australia by Capricorn Link (Australia) Pty. Ltd.
P.O. Box 704, Windsor, NSW 2756 Australia

Printed in China
Sterling ISBN 0-8069-2963-4

Acknowledgements

I heartily thank my editor, Mickey Baskett, for making this book possible and for all her wonderful expertise and support. And to all the companies who generously contributed materials used in the projects, I extend my utmost gratitude.

All Night Media
P.O. Box 10607
San Rafael, CA 94912
415/459-3013
www.allnight
media.com

American Traditional
Stencils
442 First New
Hampshire Turnpike
Northwood, NH
03261-3401
03/942-8100
www.Amtradstencil.com

Artifacts
P.O. Box 903
Palestine, TX 75802-3399
903/729-4178

Christy Crafts
P.O. Box 492
Hindsdale, IL 60521
630/323-6505

Delta Technical
Coatings, Inc.
2550 Pellissier Place
Whittier, CA 90601-1505
860/243-0303
www.deltacrafts.com

FPC Corporation
355 Hollow Hill Drive
Wauconda, IL 60084
847/487-4583

Fiskars Inc.
7811 W. Stewart Ave.
Wausau, WI 54402-8027
715/842-2091
www.fiskars.com

Jacquard Products/Rupert,
Gibbon & Spider, Inc.
800/442-0455
www.jacquardproducts.com

Krylon Products Group
31500 Solon Rd.
Solon, OH 44139
800-4-KRYLON
www.krylon.com

Loose Ends
P.O. Box 20310
Keizer, OR 97307
503/390-7457
www.4loosends.com

McGill, Inc.
131 E. Prairie St.
Marengo, IL 60152
800/982-9884
www.mcgillinc.com

Paper Adventures
2738 South 13th Street
Milwaukee, WI 53215
414/383-0414
www.paperadventures.com

Personal Stamp Exchange
360 Sutton Place
Santa Rosa, CA 95407
705/588-8058

Plaid Enterprises
3225 Westech Drive
Norcross, GA 30092
770/932-8200
www.plaidonline.com

Rubber Stampede, Inc.
967 Stanford Ave.
Oakland, CA 94608
800/NEAT-FUN

About the Author

Cindy Gorder is a professional graphic artist and designer of craft projects. She lives in rural Wisconsin on the dairy farm her husband owns and operates.

Dedication

This book is dedicated to my husband for his unwavering support and enthusiasm, my parents who taught me to be fearlessly creative, my sister who is my self-appointed cheerleader, and my craft designing "sisters" who teach, inspire, encourage, and challenge me every step of the way.

Contents

A handmade card is a treasure.

Nothing is as personal or as special as taking the time to create a one-of-a-kind card. In this book, you'll see, step-by-step, how to create more than 50 beautiful cards for all occasions, including birthdays, holidays, weddings, graduations, and baby showers. All can be made in one afternoon or less.

Making a greeting card can be as simple as cutting a piece of beautiful paper and inserting a piece of writing paper. The card (above, left) is lovely and personal, yet takes only minutes. The flower basket card (above, right) goes a few steps further. A piece of handmade paper with embedded dried flowers was cut to the card size. A flower basket sticker was applied to a piece of ecru paper and cut into a square. A ribbon attached the flower basket piece to the main card. A piece of writing paper was cut to the card size and inserted inside the card for adding a message. Even cards this simple send a message, "I care enough to send you a beautiful handmade card."

This book also includes information on supplies and tools used in card-making and basic instructions on the various decorative techniques for creating cards, such as collage, stamping, beading, silk painting, and stenciling. In addition, you'll learn basic construction techniques for cards and envelopes.

Expect most of your handmade cards to exceed the standard first class 1-oz. postage fee. Make sure to weigh the card and envelope together and apply the proper postage – you don't want it coming back to you with that unsightly "insufficient postage" stamped all over it, while the intended recipient thinks you forgot to send it! If in doubt, your postal clerk is the expert! ❑

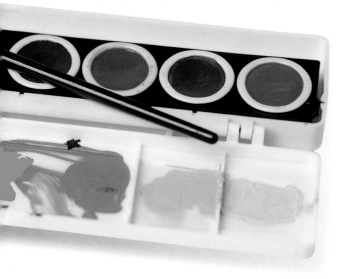

Supplies & Tools

What types of papers are best for card-making? How can I find tools to create fancy decorative edges on my cards and envelopes? This section includes information on papers, cutting and folding tools, adhesives, and supplies for coloring and decorating. You'll learn about what's available, where to shop for supplies, and how to choose the most appropriate materials and tools for your projects.

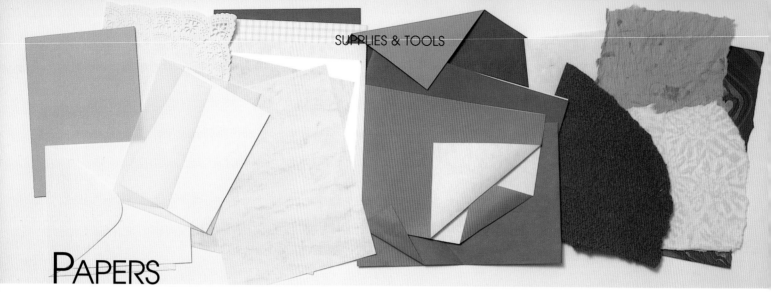

PAPERS

Papers are the foundation of cards, and there is an infinite selection from which to choose. As long as you can cut or tear and fold it, any paper can be used to make a card. The method you use to decorate the paper is the main consideration for your paper choice.

Beyond the foundation, papers can be used to decorate cards and envelopes. When you mix and match different papers and paper elements, the possibilities are truly endless.

Purchased Cards

Certainly the most convenient way to make a card is to start with a purchased card – a pre-cut blank that usually comes with an envelope. Card blanks come in a huge array of sizes, shapes, colors, textures, and finishes. Most are suitable for a variety of decorating techniques, but it's always a good idea to test your technique. You can purchase card blanks and envelopes at crafts stores, rubber stamp shops, and stores that sell art supplies and office supplies.

Card & Paper Stock

Print and copy shops have a vast selection of card stock papers that are very reasonably priced. Many lines of papers offered by professional printers include matching envelopes. If not, consider purchasing coordinating papers in text (not card) weights to make your envelopes.

A print shop is an excellent source for large sheets of paper, ideal for making accordion-fold or oversized cards. For cards with several layers, consider lighter-weight papers.

Most papers carried by print and copy shops are suitable for imprinting with a laser printer or copier, in addition to stamping and other methods of applying decoration and lettering. Other sources for papers are art supply stores, rubber stamp shops, and craft retailers.

Two-Tone Papers

Two-tone papers were used to create some of the cards in this book. These are papers that are a different color on each side. In the supply lists, the colors for both sides are listed and separated by a slash mark: [color]/[color]. Two-tone papers may be card stock or paper weight.

Handmade Papers

Handmade papers can be used for an entire card or to embellish a blank card. You can create extraordinary, one-of-a-kind cards easily by incorporating handmade papers. Many contain dried botanicals or other interesting elements. Some are beautifully marbled or silk-screened with a design. They are usually more porous and sometimes thicker – but not necessarily heavier – than standard card stock.

With the unique properties of handmade papers, it is important to test any decorating technique you intend to use. They are not recommended for use with laser-printers and copying machines. Try tearing (rather than cutting) the edges of handmade paper components to give your entire card an elegant, hand-rendered effect.

Handmade papers are available at art, craft and stamp shops or through mail order. They may be offered in stationery-size or wrapping-paper size sheets.

Vellums

Vellums are translucent papers. The most common is uncolored and is frequently offered in the form of purchased card blanks with envelopes. Vellums are versatile and elegant; they should be a basic component of your card-making supplies. Vellum is available in a rainbow of colors and many printed designs. I've found embossed vellums that are quite striking.

The surface of vellum tends to be slightly waxy, making some inks unsuitable because they won't dry. Vellum can be imprinted by most laser printers and copiers and stamped or marked with dye-based inks. Vellum accepts acrylic paint very well. Stamping with pigment inks works if you then heat-emboss (otherwise the inks never seem to dry, only to smear.) I've had success stamping with acrylic paints.

Adhesives will show through vellum, so if you can't hide your glue with stickers or appliques, punch small decorative shapes from double-sided adhesive to attach vellum just at the corners.

Use vellums for wonderful envelopes that showcase your handmade card creations. It's widely available at craft and stamp shops.

Velveteen Papers

Velveteen papers are beautiful and sumptuous. Their look and feel can't be achieved with any other paper. They can be stamped, although the design will look somewhat muted. I like them for backgrounds, frames, and decorative elements.

Embossed Papers

Embossed papers are an easy way to add textural interest. Many colors and embossed designs are available at craft and stamp stores. Embossed handmade papers and wallpapers can provide exceptionally striking impact to your cards.

Printed Papers & Wrapping Paper

Decorative papers are so readily available that you may need nothing else to create stunning cards. Printed sheets (available in the memory section of craft and stamp shops) are generally 8-1/2" x 11" or 12" x 12" and colorfully printed on one side, white on the other. Use the whole sheet or cut out motifs to use for embellishing.

Sources for decorative papers and wrapping paper include card shops, grocery stores, paper outlets, and gift shops.

Corrugated Papers

Corrugated and waffle papers provide instant texture. They are available in a rainbow of colors and a variety of ridge widths and patterns.

Wallpaper

Wallpaper can be purchased by the roll at home improvement centers and decorating stores. For a variety of smaller pieces, ask for outdated sample books. They contain beautiful papers and usually are free for the asking.

Photocopies

You can create your own colored paper with photos, cut-out images, or other flat objects, such as flowers and leaves, by photocopying them on a color copier. I recommend you arrange the images on an 8-1/2" x 11" or 11" x 17" sheet of paper and secure them in place before taking them to a copy shop. Keep in mind that most copiers have reducing and enlarging capabilities.

Decorative Specialty Papers

Specialty papers and materials are generally used for decoration and embellishment rather than an entire card. Visit the scrapbooking section of your crafts or department store, and you'll find lots of paper materials suitable for cards. Here are some of my favorites:

• Stardust papers are glitzy and tactile – use for backgrounds and accents.

• Decoupage papers include revivals of lovely vintage prints, trimmed and ready to be glued to your card.

• Tissue paper comes in colors, prints, and pearlized finishes. Wet glues can alter the color, so use double-sided tape or spray adhesives with tissues for best results.

• Old cards are a great source of images and messages. Recycle the cards you've received by cutting out elements and using them on your own creations.

• Magazine photos and graphics can be used as decorative elements, but don't overlook the colorful backgrounds that sometimes fill most of the page – they're great for decoupage and collage cards.

• Laser and die-cut elements created for scrapbooking – some on plain colored papers and some with elaborate printed designs – are great for framing other elements.

• Paper doilies and foil trims will give your creations elegance and a feminine touch.

• Paper napkins come with an array of images and colors that can be used like any other paper motif. Be sure to separate the layers and just use the top printed layer. Treat it like tissue and use appropriate adhesives.

• Clip art can be copied (and enlarged or reduced at the same time) on white or colored paper. Add color with markers, paint, or colored pencils.

• Fake fur sheets are similar to felt, but have a nap and feel that's almost real. They are a fun, funky, "touchy-feely" embellishment.

• Moving images film is available in sheets. Remember those images that changed into something else when you looked at them from a different angle? These sheets of colored film give the same effect.

• Metallic and hologram foils and films can make a card shimmer and sparkle. They're great for kids. Many are adhesive-backed. They're also available on tape rolls. ❑

CUTTING & MEASURING TOOLS

A visit to the scrapbooking section of your craft store will reveal many options for cutting and measuring paper. You need just a few basics, but you may wish to add others. Tools can be real time-savers and add visual interest to the edges of your paper elements.

Scissors

A good, **standard-sized scissors** is probably my most-used tool. A **small scissors with very sharp points** is indispensable for cutting out small shapes for collage or applique.
Decorative scissors or paper edgers are wonderful for adding interesting and elegant edges to your card. There are a vast variety of decorative designs available for paper edging.

Craft Knife

The one tool (besides scissors) that you must have is a craft knife. Sharp blades are essential. Do not be stingy with replacement blades! A sharp blade will cut through card stock or paper with a single stroke and slight pressure. If you find yourself exerting excess pressure or having to re-cut, you are working with a dull blade. As soon as you feel the paper resisting the blade, change it.

Ruler

A metal or metal-edge ruler, at least 12" long (18" is better), is necessary for cutting straight edges with your knife. If you use an inexpensive plastic ruler, the knife will soon make nicks and gouges that defeat the ruler's ability to make a perfectly straight line.

A thick, see-through **quilter's ruler** is a wonderful tool for both cutting and measuring, but it's a bit more costly. If your budget allows, a ruler made of 1/4" thick clear acrylic, with a right-angle grid, is ideal for both cutting and measuring. Get one that's at least 12" long.

Paper Cutters

Paper cutters or trimmers, with a sliding or swing-action blade, can save lots of time when cutting basic squares and rectangles. Some types have interchangeable rotary blades for creating a variety of decorative edges.

Corner Cutters

Corner cutters will allow you to make professional-looking rounded or decorative corners on your card, as well as on individual components.

Punches

Punches range from the basic to the extravagant. You can achieve many different looks very quickly with punches, and they're fun to use. Some look like the ones we used in school and punch a small shape, usually 1/4" in size or less. You can use the punched out shapes as embellishments. Larger punches come in a myriad of shapes and designs.

It takes some practice to control exactly where the punch will occur. If you are able to remove the lid of the reservoir, you'll be able to better see where the punch is positioned. Turn them over to see where the cut will be positioned on the paper. Some are designed with a longer "reach" so you can punch farther in from the edge of the paper; others will allow you to only punch 1/4" or so in from the edge.

Rotary Cutters

These tools are handy for making a long, continuous cut when used with a metal or quilter's straight edge. Interchangeable blades allow you to cut perforated lines and wavy and other decorative edges, but it's best not to use a straight edge with them.

Circle Cutters

No matter how carefully you try, it can be difficult to cut a professional-looking circle with a knife or scissors. Circle cutters solve that, with adjustable arms that can cut (or draw) perfect circles in any size you wish, from 1" to 8" in diameter. A similar tool allows you to draw or cut perfect ovals.

Cutting Mat

A self-healing cutting mat protects your work surface and helps extend the life of your blades. Most mats have a measuring grid – a most useful bonus. If you don't have a cutting mat, protect your work surface with heavy chipboard or matte board and change it often. Old cuts can make the knife blade veer off course and ruin an otherwise smooth slice.

Crimping & Embossing Tools

Crimping and embossing add dimensional designs or patterns to papers. Crimped and embossed papers can be used as is or highlighted with color on the raised areas. Some crimping and embossing tools make wavy flutes or repeating shapes, such as hearts, in the paper.

The most common crimping tool puts a series of evenly spaced grooves in the paper, much like the flutes in corrugated box material, adding dimension and texture to even the most ordinary papers. Keep in mind that crimping will shorten the paper, so allow for that or trim the paper to size after it has been crimped. *Tip:* You can get interesting results by sending lightweight foil or

wire through a standard crimping tool. (**Never** use wire heavy enough to damage the tool.)

Not all papers behave the same when they are embossed, so be sure to test small scraps before embossing a larger piece. Embossing may not add much enhancement to highly figured papers and can damage or tear some heavy papers.

Bone Folder

An important tool in paper crafting. It is formed from bone and used to fold sharp creases. A bone folder will not scratch the paper as a plastic one might. An 8" size with a point is best.

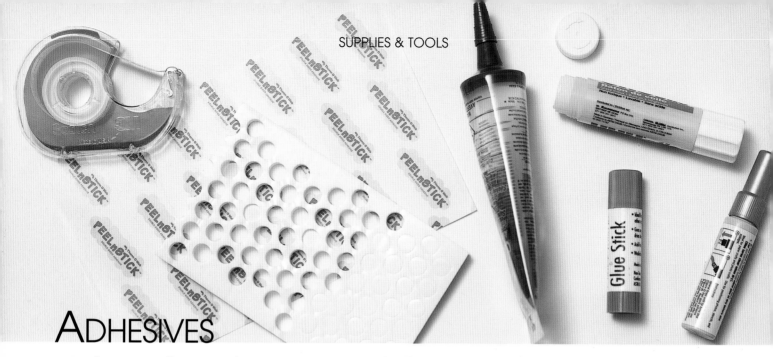

ADHESIVES

With so many adhesives on the market, it's pretty easy to find the one that's appropriate for just about any application. You'll need a few different kinds of adhesives, as there's not one universal glue for everything. A well-stocked scrapbooking department will have several types to choose from.

I like to use the least messy, least bulky, and quickest drying adhesive that my work will allow. This varies from one situation to the next, depending on the materials I'm using. Here are a few favorites.

Double-sided, Dry Adhesives

(Double-stick tape is one.) These are quick and accessible but are sometimes a little too bulky for sheer papers; they are best used for small areas. Double-sided sheet adhesives can be cut to any size and shape you need. They have a paper liner on each side. You first peel away the liner from one side and apply it to one of your surfaces, then remove the second liner to attach the second surface. This adhesive comes in permanent and repositionable. Save and use the small scraps – nothing goes to waste.

Another type of dry adhesive comes in a dispenser and is rolled on the back of your paper. This one's handy for straight edges, but can be a bit tricky to control (at least the 1/2" wide product is), and it's permanent, so you can't undo a mistake. I like it, though, because it's not at all bulky and doesn't show through sheer papers, such as tissue. (It will show through vellum, however.)

Glue Pens and Sticks

A liquid archival glue in a bottle with a small applicator tip (like a marker) is a good choice for getting adhesive on small shapes and for sticking paper to paper. It dries fairly quickly, is permanent when dry, and repositionable while still wet. The drawbacks are that it isn't always strong enough to hold every kind of applique and doesn't work well on extremely porous surfaces. (It soaks in too much.) Try it. If it doesn't hold, you can always resort to a different adhesive.

Glue sticks are another handy way to stick things together, especially paper to paper. They work with just about any kind of paper, dry fairly quickly, and are easy to apply.

Jeweler's Glue

Used for attaching unusual objects, such as charms, wire, or buttons. Get one that dries clear and sticks to all kinds of surfaces, particularly glass and metal. It should hold just about anything you want. Use sparingly to keep your project looking tidy.

Dimensional Dots

These are made of foam that has adhesive on both sides. It's a way to give an element extra dimension and hold it to the paper at the same time. Dimensional dots are generally used for paper to paper adhesion, although other lightweight objects may work. For less dimension, double-sided foam carpet tape can be easily cut to fit your needs. It's about half the thickness of dimensional dots and can be stacked to any height you like.

COLORING MEDIUMS

Used alone or in combination, a variety of options for adding color to your cards are at your disposal.

Ink

Whether in the form of **stamp pads or marking pens,** there are basically two kinds of ink: dye-based and pigment. *Dye-based inks* dry quickly and are suitable for most paper surfaces. *Pigment inks* dry more slowly, and can be used with embossing powders and a heat embossing tool. If used alone, test first on the paper you are using for compatibility. While pigment inks work just fine on some papers, they won't dry on most vellums and will smear, even after several days.

If you plan to tint a stamped image with markers, pay attention to the kind of ink in the markers and use the opposite type of ink to stamp the image to prevent the marker ink from lifting the stamped image during coloring.

A **brayer** is a useful tool for applying ink from a stamp pad to paper to create a colored background. *Interchangeable rollers* will allow you to create large areas of overall patterns.

Another handy ink applicator is the **dauber.** Daubers are small sponges pre-loaded with ink, similar to tiny stamp pads, mounted on pen-size barrels. Many have a different color on each end. They are especially handy for use with small stamps and stenciled areas.

You can use **stencil daubers** to apply ink as well. They are small domed sponges attached to the end of a small dowel and can be used to transfer ink from a stamp pad to paper. They are perfect for use with small stencils. Simply tap the sponge end against the stamp pad to load, then tap over a stencil opening to transfer the ink to the paper.

Paint

Acrylic paints, generally sold in 2 oz. bottles at crafts stores, are ideal for decorating cards. Be aware, however, that the moisture in the paint may cause ripples, buckles, or other slight distortions to your paper, which may be a desirable or undesirable result, depending on your preference. When the paint dries, the distortion may subside dramatically. Some acrylic paints are specially formulated to use with paper and cause little or no distortion. You can't predict the final outcome without testing, so always test acrylics on the specific paper you are using to make sure you will like the results.

Watercolor paints are useful for tinting and achieving a painterly effect. Like acrylics, they may affect some papers adversely, so test first.

Some of my favorite paints for cards are the **metallic "leafing pens"** that have a marker-type nib and are filled with bright, shiny, lustrous paint in gold, silver, or copper. The ink dries quickly and is super for gilding the edges of cards and envelope flaps.

Colored Pencils

There is no mess or chance of an accidental spill with colored pencils, and the results can be as spectacular as any paint or marker technique. They are ideal for use with stamped images and stencils and to enhance painted areas.

If the only colored pencils you've used are the ones you had in grade school, you are in for a pleasant surprise. *Artist-quality colored pencils* are sold in craft and art supply stores individually and in sets. They are very easy to apply and the color transfers cleanly and smoothly. It's quite easy to control the intensity by applying light or heavy pressure. Shading and blending is easy.

DECORATING MATERIALS

This is a sampling of the decorating options available.

Rubber Stamps

Stamped images can be applied to paper with ink, markers, paint, and embossing powders (my favorite).

For embossing with powders, you will need either pigment (slow-drying) ink or clear embossing "ink," embossing powder, and a heat tool. Embossing powders are not all equal. Some are coarser than others. If your stamp is very detailed, choose a very fine embossing powder. You'll also need a heat gun (much hotter and less "windy" than a hair dryer). If you are sensitive to noise, look for a quiet one.

Stencils

Stencils are an excellent way to get an image on paper quickly and easily. Use with acrylic paint, stencil creams or gels, ink daubers, colored pencils, or stamping ink.

When applying paint, stencil creams or gels, or ink from a stamp pad, choose a stencil brush size that corresponds with the size of the openings of the stencil. To apply large stenciled images, consider using a stencil roller or a small painter's touch-up roller.

Leaf & Foil

These products are commonly sold in gold, but other metal colors are readily available. Leaf or composition leaf is feather-light and will stick to wet paint or a specially made adhesive. It may tarnish, with time, unless a protective sealer is applied. (Sealing is not generally necessary for greeting cards.)

Foil is transferred from a carrier sheet to a specific adhesive and is very shiny. It is very attractive, but looks more artificial than leaf, especially when used in large solid areas. Foil is quite pleasing when used in broken, random patterns or for lettering. It will also stick to adhesive that has been extruded from a hot glue gun and allowed to cool, yielding a dimensional result.

Fabric Paints

Fabric paints are somewhat dimensional, often include glitter or pearlized highlights, and generally come in a bottle that has a very fine applicator tip. Use this paint to create, highlight, or outline images and words, draw borders, make background dots, and adhere beads.

Glitter Glue

As the name implies, this is glue with glitter suspended in it. You can get it in bottles or in pen-size containers – both come with applicator tips. Write or draw with it for jazzy effects.

Stickers

There are stickers for sale everywhere – card and gift shops, the grocery store, and all the craft and stamp outlets. They come in every theme imaginable. You can make your own from sticker paper (available from rubber stamping suppliers), using rubber stamps or stencils and cutting out the desired shape.

Stickers provide a quick, effective way to decorate a card and a good way to attach vellum panels or cover up adhesives that can show through vellums or other thin or translucent papers.

Foam & Sponge Stamps

These type of stamps can only be used with paint. The paint is applied with a brush to the stamp surface. Design images are usually larger than rubber stamps. See page 24 for technique.

Beads

Add dimension and interest by gluing on seed beads to accent and embellish a design. For the glue, use fabric paint – the applicator tip makes it easy to apply just a tiny dot of paint in which to set each bead. When the paint dries, it becomes part of the design; it doesn't have to be "invisible" like other adhesives.

Make tasseled accents of strands of beads on thread or wire and attach to the card.

Wire

Use a lightweight wire (18 or 24 gauge) that you can bend easily with your fingers. Round-nose pliers and cutting pliers are useful tools to use with wire, but you can get by with household needlenose pliers in a pinch.

Wire is available in many colors and can be used as a stand-alone decorative element or as a way to attach other decorative elements, such as buttons, beads, and charms.

Silk Painting

Silk painting is easier than you might think and a very personal way to enhance a special card. Use silk dyes for vivid colors (add water for pastel shades) or watercolor paints for softer, more diluted effects. Use brushes and apply the colors randomly. Embellish the design with markers, then dab with a small, wet brush to diffuse the lines.

Charms, Buttons & What-nots

If it's fairly flat, it's probably a candidate for embellishing a card! Some options include broken or outdated jewelry, ribbons, buttons, dried flowers – whatever. These odds and ends can make your card unlike any other.

Creative Techniques

*This section discusses a variety of creative techniques that can be used to create and embellish your cards. The techniques are arranged alphabetically, from beading to wiring. Each technique is represented by a symbol. **You'll find these technique icons included in the instructions for individual card projects** to use to reference the techniques in this section. Options for adding lettering to create messages for your cards are also discussed.*

Always practice a new technique or tool on scrap paper before using it on your project.

Beading ○

Small beads are flat enough to use on cards and can be quite dramatic. Attach them however you like, using glue, thread, or wire. When you use thread or wire, stitch or wire right through the front of the card and cover the "tails" on the back side with another panel of paper.

If you are doing other decorative treatments to the card, do the others first and save the bead application for last.

Supplies

Small beads in assorted sizes and colors
Fabric paint (to use as glue) and needle tool
or beading needle and thread
or fine wire and needle tool

Glue method

1. To secure each bead, apply a small dot of fabric paint to the card (you can do up to 10 at a time) and then set a bead in each dot of wet paint. Use a needle tool to maneuver the bead so it's sitting on edge and pushed all the way into the paint. Take care not to bump beads that have been positioned as you add more.
2. When all beads are in place, set the whole card aside to dry for several hours.
3. Check for any loose beads. Re-glue the ones that aren't secure.

Thread method

1. Using a threaded beading needle, string beads on thread and stitch them to the card.
2. Knot securely on the back side. For extra security, tape or glue the knots before trimming the thread tails.
3. Cover the knots on the back with an additional panel of paper, paper appliques, or stickers.

1. Applying dots of fabric paint as a glue to hold beads.

2. Placing beads in paint dots with a needle tool.

Wire method

1. String beads on wire, leaving at least 2" of wire at each end.
2. With a needle tool, poke small holes through the paper and insert the wire tails to the back. Secure by twisting the tails together if they are long enough. If the tails don't meet, twist each one into a flat spiral and secure to the back of the card with tape.
3. Cover the back of the card with an additional paper, paper appliques, or stickers.

3. Stringing beads on thread.

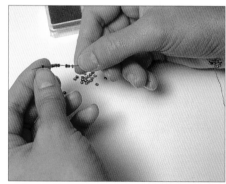

4. Stringing beads on wire.

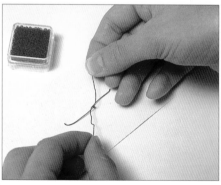

5. Twisting wire tails together on the back of a card.

Collage & Layering

My dictionary describes collage as "an artistic composition of materials and objects pasted over a surface...." That pretty much covers it. Most of the cards in this book are collages – some very basic, some more complex. Layering is a type of collage that uses layers of paper for a decorative effect. All the layers are visible when the final layer is placed; most often the layers form borders or "frames" for the layer that follows.

Being flat enough and lightweight enough are the only limitations I can think of for items to include in a collage. A collage might be just layers of papers or might start with papers and include charms, old postage stamps, buttons, wire, ticket stubs, or flattened bottle caps. There's no limit and no rules, making it a perfect medium to personalize a greeting.

Use the adhesive that is most appropriate for each element of your collage – you may need to use them all at different stages of your composition.

1. Trying out the arrangement of a collage.

Supplies

Any or all may be incorporated.
Papers for color and shape
Paper images (clip art, stamped images, photos, magazine clips, stickers, parts of other greeting cards)
Paper ephemera (ticket stubs, birth announcements, baseball cards, postage stamps or color photocopies of any of these)
Three-dimensional materials (dried botanicals, miniatures, ribbons, wire, beads, charms, buttons, feathers, stickers)

Basic Collage Method

1. Start with a card foundation. Lay out all your materials and try different arrangements until you find one you like. It doesn't have to be exact at this point – you are just deciding what to include and what to save for another project.
2. Build your collage layer by layer, using adhesives appropriate to each connection. Try to avoid adding

bulk, but ensure the adhesion between the layers is strong enough to hold as successive layers are added. If necessary, set aside so each layer can dry before proceeding to the next.

Option: Objects may be wired or sewn on the face of the card as an alternative to gluing. Use the techniques discussed on the beading page.

Basic Layering Method

1. Start with a card foundation. Try different combinations of papers until you arrive at an arrangement that pleases you.
2. Cut out the papers, making each successive layer smaller that the preceding one.
3. Glue the layers, using adhesives appropriate to each connection. Ensure the adhesion between the layers is strong enough to hold as successive layers are added. If necessary, set aside so each layer can dry before proceeding to the next.

2. Gluing the elements of the collage, layer by layer.

Leafing & Foiling ✳

Nothing dresses up a card like a bit of shimmer! The basic idea is to apply an adhesive agent to the area to be treated, then apply the leaf or foil. Use leaf and foil to highlight designs or create shapes.

Supplies for Leafing

Gold, silver, or copper composition leaf
Composition leaf adhesive
Soft brush
Optional: Leaf sealer

Basic Leafing Method

Because leaf is almost lighter than air, it will stick to the slightest amount of tack. You may wish to experiment with other sticking agents, such as double-sided dry adhesives, paint, or even fabric paint and work with the one that suits you.

1. Apply leaf adhesive to the area to be leafed. Let dry until the adhesive is clear but still slightly tacky.
2. Cut the leaf, along with its liner paper, into squares approximately 2" x 2". Handle the leaf by the paper to avoid having it stick to your fingers.
3. Carefully slide the leaf off the liner paper and onto the adhesive.
4. Pat in place with a soft brush.
5. Carefully brush away "crumbs" and excess leaf.
6. *Option:* To prevent the leaf from ever tarnishing, apply sealer. (For greeting cards, I don't seal.)

Alternative: Paint Method

Paint can be used as an adhesive.
1. Apply paint to surface.
2. Apply leafing to paint while paint is still wet.
3. Rub with soft brush to adhere. Brush away excess leaf.

Continued on next page

1. Applying leaf adhesive with a brush.

3. Patting leaf into place.

2. Sliding leaf onto adhesive.

4. Applying leaf to a large area.

Leafing (cont.)

Alternative: Dry Transfer Method

Use a special rub-on adhesive that is sold in sheets – many are available in shapes and designs.

1. Rub adhesive on paper with a craft stick to transfer.
2. Apply the leaf.
3. Rub with soft brush to adhere. Brush away excess leaf.

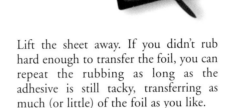

Supplies for Foiling

Metallic foil (gold, silver, or other color)
Foil adhesive and bristle paint brush
or cool temp glue gun

Basic Foiling Methods

Foils will stick to the special adhesives formulated for them as well as to other "sticky" or "tacky" surfaces, such as the adhesive extruded from a glue gun (to yield dimensional designs) or some dry, double-sided tapes. Experiment to see what method you like.

Foil adhesive method

1. Use a brush to apply foil adhesive. The adhesive can be applied heavily for a solid foiled area or lightly for a more subtle result. Let dry until the adhesive is clear but still tacky.
2. Place the foil, dull side down, against the adhesive and rub firmly with your finger.

Lift the sheet away. If you didn't rub hard enough to transfer the foil, you can repeat the rubbing as long as the adhesive is still tacky, transferring as much (or little) of the foil as you like.

3. Brush away excess with a soft brush.

Glue gun method

1. Sketch a simple design or pattern with a pencil on the surface to be foiled.
2. Apply a thread of glue from a low-temp gun to the pencil lines. Let the glue cool until cloudy and firm.
3. Lay the dull side of the foil against the glue bead and rub with your fingers (or bone folder) to transfer the foil to the top and sides of the bead of glue.

Instant Foil Lettering

The instant gilded lettering used on some cards in this book is sold in sets. The adhesive is printed on a carrier sheet in the shape of the letters along with small sheets of foil. Follow the manufacturer's directions to apply this type of foiling.

1. Applying adhesive with a brush to highlight a ridged paper.

2. Transferring foil.

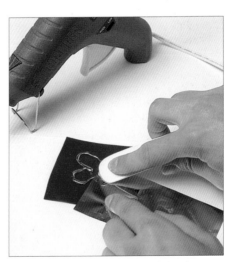

3. Transferring foil to a bead of glue from a low-temp glue gun.

Painting with Stamps ✿

Paint is a universal material for applying decorative elements to just about everything, and cards are no exception. Even if you don't have any previous painting experience, you can still use paint effectively to enhance your cards. In this book paint is used almost exclusively with sponge stamps.

Sponges and stamps are quick, easy ways to apply paint and get professional-looking results. Sponge stamps are available in a wide variety of shapes and sizes. Compressed sponges are blanks from which to cut your own shapes. Foam stamps are available in a wide variety of shapes and sizes, generally with more intricate detail than sponge stamps but not as detailed as rubber stamps. It is possible to use foam stamps with ink rather than paint, but they are designed for paint and will provide very satisfying results with little or no practice.

Be sure to clean your sponges and stamps thoroughly before putting them away; dried-on paint will ruin them.

3. Setting the sponge on the surface.

Supplies

Acrylic paint
Sponge stamps or compressed sponges
or foam stamps and sponge wedges
Palette (some wax paper or a plastic or
   foam plate will do)

Basic Method for sponge stamps and compressed sponges

1. Squeeze a puddle of paint on your palette. Dip a sponge stamp or prepared compressed sponge shape into the paint. Move or dab the sponge to load it with an even coverage of paint.
2. Set the paint-loaded sponge on the surface, applying very little pressure.
3. Lift the sponge straight up to reveal the image.

Basic Method for foam stamps

1. Squeeze a small puddle of paint on a palette. Use a sponge wedge such as a makeup applicator to evenly apply paint to the foam stamp.
2. While paint is still wet, position the stamp on your paper and apply even pressure to transfer the paint to the surface.
3. Lift the stamp straight up to reveal a perfect image. If your image isn't perfect, adjust the amount of paint you load on the stamp, and try again.

1. Drawing a design on a compressed sponge.

4. Applying paint to a foam stamp with a sponge wedge.

2. Dipping the sponge shape in paint.

5. Pressing foam stamp to surface.

Paper-Pricking

A Victorian craft revived, paper pricking is an easy and elegant method of creating a soft, subtle design on paper. The effect depends on which side of the paper the needle was pushed into – a raised design is created by pricking from back to front, a smooth design is pricked from front to back. A pricked design will show up best if placed over a contrasting background paper.

A stencil is an ideal source for a pattern, but you can also use a design drawn or printed on paper. The pricked holes should be uniformly spaced. The size of the hole is determined by how far you push the needle tool into the paper. If you wish, perforate a part of the design from the opposite side of the paper.

To protect your work surface when paper-pricking, work on a 1/4" to 1/2" thick foundation of foam core or craft foam. Stack layers, if necessary, to achieve this thickness. Beneath this, use a self-healing mat or a piece of cardboard.

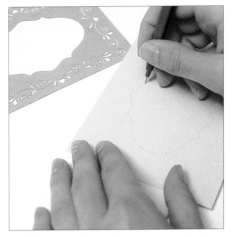

2. Using a needle tool to create a pricked design.

Supplies

Card stock or paper
Needle tool
or #5 sharp sewing needle pushed eye-first
  into a cork
Stencil or design on paper

Basic Method

1. Position the stencil or drawn design on the card. Tape, if desired, to hold in place.
2. Use the needle tool to perforate the design.

Freeform Method

Use freeform paper pricking (without stencil or pattern) to enhance cuts made with decorative edgers and punches – simply mimic the pattern created by the cut or punched shape.

1. Using a stencil to trace a design for pricking. Or you can prick inside the stencil opening.

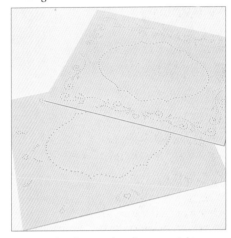

3. Completed examples of paper-pricking.

Photo Images

Everyone loves receiving cards made from photos. With color copies of a handful of your favorite photos, you can create very personal greeting cards.

Be sure to use photocopies of your photos rather than originals or prints on photographic paper. Photocopies are lighter in weight and easier to handle, and most copiers have enlarging and reducing capabilities and can make copies on a variety of papers, giving you further creative options.

Black and white photos reproduce better on color copiers than on black toner copiers. If you find a place with a high-end copier and a knowledgeable operator, you can have them adjust the color to look like old sepia-toned prints. Or get really creative and turn them into any color you like! Imagine a black-and-white photo of a daisy copied in blue on pastel pink paper. Add embellishments to make a special card for a very special recipient.

Basic Method

1. Copy photo on paper, using a photocopier. Enlarge or reduce image to fit your card.
2. Crop or cut out image and glue to card.
3. Embellish.

Wedding Photo Card

Size: 5-3/4" x 4-1/2"

Techniques:

Supplies

Paper:
Metallic paper, gold, 5-3/4" x 9"
Card stock, purple, 5-1/2" x 8-1/2"
Writing paper, 5-3/4" x 9"
Photocopy of wedding photo

Decorative Elements:
Stencil, rose design
Stencil paint, gold
Metal frame, gold, 3-1/4" x 2-1/4"

Tools & Other Supplies:
Stencil brush
Glue stick
Glue gun and glue sticks *or* jewelry glue

Step-by-Step

1. Score and fold all pieces of paper (except photo) at centers of longest length. Fold and smooth creases with the bone folder.
2. Mark the area in the center of the purple card stock where frame will be placed. Set frame aside.
3. Stencil a design using gold paint on the purple card stock outside of the area where the frame will be. Allow to dry.
4. With the glue stick, attach the purple card stock to the outside of the gold paper, creating an even border on all sides.
5. Attach photo, then frame to front of card, using hot glue or jewelry glue.
6. Insert writing paper. This piece can be loose or can be attached at fold to gold paper with small dots of glue. ❑

Gold on Gold Photo Card

Open size: 10" x 7"
Folded size: 5" x 7"

Techniques:

Supplies

Paper:
Purchased card, harvest gold
Card stock, lighter shade of gold, 4-1/2" x 6-1/2"
Card stock, any color, one sheet

Decorative Elements:
3 color copied photos in sizes from 1-3/4" square to 3" square
Leafing pen, gold
Stencils - heart, ribbons, borders
Stencil paint, gold

Tools & Other Supplies:
Circle cutter
Corner cutting scissors
Stencil brush
Glue stick or glue pen

Step-by-Step

1. With the circle cutter, cut scrap paper circles to determine the appropriate size for each photo.
2. Use scrap circles to determine the position of circles on card front. To mark, fold circle in quarters and find center. Position folded circle on lighter gold card stock. Make a pencil mark on the card stock. Align needle of circle cutter to dot.

Continued on next page

26

Gold on Gold (cont.)

3. Cut openings in the separate sheet of harvest gold card stock.

4. Set the circle cutter to make circles 1/8" wider than the photo frames, and cut from "any color" piece of card stock to make an embossing template.

5. Position the circle template around a photo frame and mark with embossing tool. Keeping the template and frame aligned, flip over and emboss from the back of the card stock, following the first mark you made with the stylus. Do this for each of the three openings in the gold card.

6. Use a gold leafing pen to decorate the raised embossed frames with broken lines.

7. Position the photos behind the frame openings. Attach with glue.

8. Use corner cutters to round each corner of the framed photo panel.

9. Use a leafing pen to make gold checks around the edges of the folded card front.

10. Glue the photo panel to the center of the card front. ❑

Rubber Stamping & Embossing

A vast array of results can be achieved by a few different stamping techniques. Simply changing the ink and paper colors can completely change the final result. Add embossing powders and you've greatly multiplied your stamping opportunities.

Embossing powders are made of tiny granules, and some powders are coarser than others. Try to match the size of the granules to the amount of detail in the stamp for the most pleasing results. Finer powders, sometimes referred to as "detail embossing powders," are best for enhancing a delicately rendered stamp.

It takes some practice to know precisely where the image will land, so allow some flexibility in your design. Always test your stamp on scrap paper before stamping your card. When you have achieved the image on scrap paper, proceed to the card. Use a stamp cleaner to clean your stamps.

3. Applying embossing powder to a stamped image.

Supplies

Rubber stamps
Ink pad *or* ink dauber
Alternative: Marking pens
Embossing ink *or* pigment ink
Embossing powder
Embossing heat tool
Wax paper

Basic Stamping Method

1. Start with a clean stamp. Tap it up and down on a stamp pad to load with ink.
2. Position the stamp above but not touching the paper. When you think your stamp is properly aligned, keep it parallel to the surface, place the stamp on the paper, and apply gentle pressure. Rock it ever so slightly to ensure an even impression. Lift straight up.
3. Re-ink the stamp for each new impression.

Alternative Method: Colored Markers

An alternative to inking a stamp from a ink pad is to use markers. The image may not be as dark as one from an ink pad, but if you've properly coated the stamp, all the details will appear crisply. You can use several colors on the same stamp. Overlapping colors will give you simple shading and blending.

1. Coat the stamp completely with marker color. Huff on it to re-moisten the ink.
2. Press on the paper.

Basic Embossing Method

Embossing ink is usually clear, sometimes lightly tinted so you can see where you stamped, but not tinted enough to affect the color of the embossing powder. If you use pigment ink, the ink color may interact with embossing powder color, and you can use this to your advantage. For instance, if you don't

1. Stamping with an ink pad.

2. Inking a stamp with markers.

4. Pouring off excess embossing powder.

5. Using the heat tool to liquefy the powder and raise the image.

have red embossing powder, stamp the image with red pigment ink and emboss with clear powder. Pigment ink will dry more quickly than embossing ink, so sprinkle on the powder immediately after you have stamped the image. Whatever ink color and embossing powder you choose, the technique is the same. Place the card on a piece of wax paper that has been creased and opened back up.

1. Stamp the image on the paper with embossing ink or pigment ink.
2. While the ink is still wet (you will have plenty of time with embossing ink, less time with pigment ink), sprinkle on the embossing powder and completely cover the image.

3. Tilt the card to remove the excess powder, catching it on the wax paper. Tap the card from the back to remove stray bits of powder. Use a small soft-bristle paintbrush, if necessary, to brush away unwanted powder near the stamped image.
4. Return the excess powder to its container. Replace the cap to avoid accidentally spilling the powder.
5. Turn on the heat tool. Bring it within 6" of the powdered image. Gradually moving it closer, heat the image until all the powder has liquefied and is transformed into a glossy, raised image.

Silk Painting

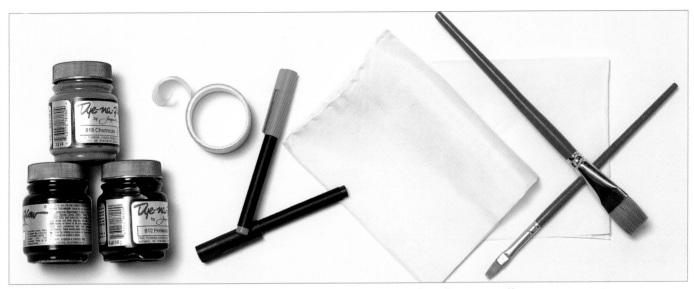

Silk painting is a beautiful, easy technique for creating one-of-a-kind cards. Dyes will give you more intense, saturated colors and can be diluted with water for pastel effects. Watercolors will look softer and more subtle.

Supplies

100% silk fabric, cut slightly larger than the finished size of the card
Silk dyes *or* watercolor paints
Medium or fine markers
Water
Soft bristle paint brushes
Freezer paper
Tape

Basic Method

1. Tape the piece of silk to the dull side of the freezer paper, stretching the silk slightly to take up the slack.
2. Load the brush with dye or paint. Touch the brush to the silk and let the liquid flow into the fabric. Drag the brush randomly to move the dye. Reload often. Notice how the color and saturation are affected by the amount of liquid you add to the brush.
3. When the entire surface of the silk is painted, lift a corner of the tape and gently blow behind the fabric to lift it from the paper. Set aside to dry.
4. If the dried silk has pulled away from the paper, remove the tape, flatten the fabric, and re-secure the fabric to the paper.
5. Draw spirals, circles, or other freeform designs on the painted silk with markers. Use a small brush, dipped in water, to diffuse the hard marker lines, if desired. Let dry.

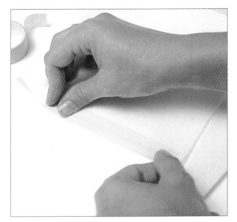

1. Taping the silk to the dull side of the freezer paper.

2. Applying dye with a brush.

3. Adding designs with a marker.

Stenciling ♥

Stenciling is a technique for transferring designs to paper. Paint, ink, or colored pencils can be used to apply color through the openings of the stencil.

Supplies

Stencil

Acrylic paint *or* stamping ink *or* colored pencils

Stencil brush, stencil dauber, or cosmetic sponge

Paper towels, folded in quarters

Low tack masking tape

Palette (A piece of wax paper or a disposable plastic or foam plate will do.)

Paint Method

1. Position the stencil on the paper. Secure with a piece of tape, if you like.
2. Squeeze small puddles of paint (about 1/2" in diameter) on a palette or a piece of wax paper. Holding the stencil brush vertically, dip the tips of the bristles in the paint. Dab off most of the paint on a paper towel.
3. Working with a very dry brush, dab or swirl the color on the paper through the openings in the stencil.
4. Reload the brush as often as necessary to complete the design.

5. Add shading colors on top of stenciled colors, if desired, while the stencil is still in place. Lift the stencil to reveal the image and allow the paint to dry completely.

Ink Method

1. Position the stencil on the paper and secure with a little tape, if you like.
2. Apply ink using a stencil dauber, sponge dauber, or cosmetic sponge through the openings of the stencil. The ink should never be runny.
3. Remove stencil. Set aside to dry completely.

Colored Pencil Method

1. Position the stencil on the paper and secure with a little tape, if you like.
2. Trace lightly inside the openings with a colored pencil. Use the light color and pressure for the outlines.
3. Remove the stencil. Color and shade the design with pencils in the colors of your choice. You can also fill in the bridges (the gaps created by the stencil configuration), if you don't want the finished design to look stenciled.

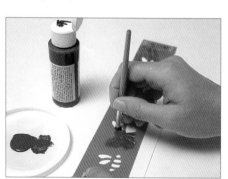

1. Stenciling with acrylic paint, using a brush.

3. Stenciling with ink, using a dauber.

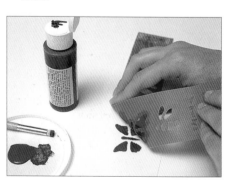

2. Lifting the stencil to reveal the image.

4. Outlining a stencil design with a colored pencil.

Stencil-Embossing

Metal stencils made specifically for embossing are easiest to work with, but just about any stencil can be used to create dramatic embossing effects. Test your paper with your stencil to see if you have a compatible match.

Clear, uncolored stencils are hard to see through opaque paper, although they can be used with vellums. Stencils made from heavy plastic may cause the paper to tear. The thicker the stencil material, the deeper the embossing will be (or, actually, the more raised it will appear when it is turned right side up).

Papers so opaque that light cannot pass through them are almost impossible to work with because you can't see the stencil. Vellums, on the other hand, are transparent enough to emboss them without the aid of a light source. While you can use a window for your light source, an inexpensive, portable light box or light table will make doing this technique much more comfortable and enjoyable.

The best stylus to use is one with two different end sizes, but just about any stylus with round ball ends will work for embossing.

1. Positioning a stencil for stencil-embossing.

Supplies:

Stencil, Paper, Stylus, Light box or light table or window (except for vellum papers)

Basic Method

1. Position the stencil wrong side down on the light box and the paper wrong side down atop the stencil. If your embossed design requires precise placement on the paper, plan this ahead and place pencil marks on the back of the paper to aid in alignment.
2. Huff on the paper to make it more receptive to the embossing process.
3. Using the stylus, trace the stencil shape on the paper. If lettering, move and re-align the stencil for each character, taking care with the positioning.
4. Leave the embossing as is or enhance by rubbing a little paint or color over the raised areas. To prevent the color from accidentally getting where you don't want it, position the stencil and use it as a mask.

2. Stencil-embossing with a stylus.

Wiring

Wire is a popular craft material and is available in many colors and thicknesses, called gauges. Thinner gauge wires that will hold a shape but can be bent easily with your fingers can be twisted and worked into striking flat embellishments. Wire also can be used to hold buttons, charms, beads, and other objects to cards.

While you can get by with a household needlenose pliers, a jeweler's round-nose pliers will allow you to make nice-looking ends and put bends in heavier wire precisely where you want them. A wire cutter is a must for the heavier gauges if you want to preserve your scissors.

Supplies

Wire, 18 to 26 gauge, Needlenose or round-nose pliers, Wire cutter

Tips for Using Wire

- Sketch out a design you like and use it as a guide to bend the wire to that shape. If the wire crosses itself, use that as an opportunity to make a twist to help keep the wire in the desired shape.
- To attach the wire to paper, either leave tails on each end that you can poke through and secure on the back side or use additional wire to make and poke loops through from the back to hold your shape in place. Keep everything as flat as possible on the back side. Use the pliers to make tight bends that are snug against the paper.
- Once the wire is secured to the paper, tape everything in place on the back. Cover the entire back with a clean panel of paper that is heavy enough to keep the wire from bumping or poking through.

Creating Messages

There are several options for getting your words on paper. The most basic is your own handwriting. If you aren't comfortable with that, practice printing your message on scrap paper and trace the message with the aid of a light box. If you have access to a computer, you can print out lettering and use it straight from the printer or trace over it with colored ink or even paint.

Have you noticed how many mass-produced cards have whimsical-looking, "handwritten" messages? They've figured out that it feels more personal to the recipient that way. Don't be too compulsive about creating perfect lettering.

Good letter spacing is the key to good-looking lettering. Computer-generated type is automatically correctly letter-spaced. If you are printing by hand, stenciling, or using stickers, notice how the letters and baselines (where the bottoms of the letter sit) look in relationship to each other. Note that lower case letters such as "g" and "y" have descenders that extend below the baseline.

Whatever method you select, take a few minutes to practice first on scrap paper. If nothing else, you will see how to space the letters and lines evenly (or how well you've inked your stamp).

Hand Lettering (1)

If the message has several lines, lightly mark evenly spaced baselines that can be erased after the lettering is done (or use a light box, with baselines marked on a separate sheet of paper). There are many books of lettering styles available in craft and scrapbooking departments. You can also copy lettering you like from books, magazines, or other cards.

Calligraphy (2)

One of the prettiest ways to write your message is to use calligraphy. There are a variety of pens and materials available in arts & craft shops as well as fine stationery stores. You can choose to use ink and pens with nibs or calligraphy markers that are ready for writing. A good calligraphy book will give hints on how to letter and usually contain alphabet examples and worksheets for practicing your technique.

Stenciled Lettering (3)

Draw a light pencil baseline. Use paint or ink with a stencil to apply entire phrases or use an alphabet stencil for individual letters. Be sure the ink or paint is dry before repositioning your stencil for the next letter; ink dries slightly faster than paint, and dye-based inks dry more quickly than pigment inks.

Stickers (4)

Stickers are available that contain pages of letters. Position each letter along your pencilled baseline. Rub lightly to adhere all the edges before erasing the pencil line.

Rub-on (Dry) Transfer Lettering (5)

Sheets of multiple, individual letters (and sometimes complete phrases) are available in art supply shops and crafts stores. These were used by graphic artists before computers to create headlines for printing jobs. Basically a dry decal, they are still available and are an ideal way to letter your cards, but you'll need a bit of practice.

Transfer lettering works like other rub-on transfers. Select lettering sheets that have a small guideline printed below each letter for easiest use.

1. Mark a light pencil guideline or baseline.
2. Position the sheet (minus its paper liner) so the guideline on the carrier sheet below your first letter lines up with the pencil line. (If your penciled baseline touches the letters, you might damage them when you try to erase the baseline.)
3. Rub directly over the letter, but not over the surrounding letters, with a pencil, stylus, or ballpoint pen, until the letter releases to the paper. Line up the next letter and repeat.

Tip: Remove unwanted letters or portions of accidentally transferred letters with a bit of tape or scratch them away with the tip of a craft knife. You can reapply letters on top of any that have portions missing.

Rubber stamping (6)

Individual letters and complete phrases are available as rubber stamps. These stamps can be used with embossing powder to create embossed stamping. For embossed handwriting, use a pen filled with embossing ink to write your message.

It can be a bit tricky to align individual stamped letters, so practice first on scrap paper. You might want to make a guideline, rather than a baseline, that is even with the bottom edge of the stamp, provided all the stamps are uniformly trimmed and mounted. Consider stamping in a whimsical, curving line rather than trying for a perfectly straight alignment.

- If you are embossing the rubber stamping, you will need to stamp and emboss each letter individually. This technique works best for stamps with complete phrases, unless you have a lot of patience!
- Embossed handwriting is fast and effective. Use an embossing-ink pen or other slow-drying ink, and write as if using a marker. Emboss, using the basic method.

Computer Lettering (7)

You can type your message on a computer and use a laser printer or inkjet printer to print your message. Computer-generated type is automatically letter-spaced and most word processing programs have a huge range of type styles available. Print your message on the paper stock before making the card or cut or tear your printed phrases and glue in place.

Inspiration for Messages

Sometimes a simple message is all that's needed – "Thank you," "I miss you," "Be my valentine," "Happy Birthday," "Merry Christmas." Other times, the occasion may call for something more elaborate or personal, or clever. If that's the case and your words fail you, try consulting a book of quotations, books of poetry (Browning, Shakespeare, e.e. cummings), lyrics from your favorite songwriters' recordings, or an inspirational text (the Bible, *The Prophet,* or any of the popular books of affirmations). Be sure to properly attribute your source.

You can also recycle greetings and messages from cards you have received. It may be possible to cut out or tear out the lettering and attach it to your card as part of a collage or decoration.

Happy Birthday

HAPPY DAYS ARE HERE AGAIN !

(5)

A timeless wish for a season of Joy

(6)

Happy Easter

(7)

A gift
for the
bride-
to-be

Happiness
always~

Love~

Cindy

May your
married life
be blessed and
charmed!

Basic Construction

This section discusses the basic techniques for constructing your cards before you decorate them and how to make envelopes. There are some important tips to learn that will make your card-making easy, and your cards will have a more professional look.

Preparing your workspace is one of the most important aspects of crafting. Set aside a special area for your crafting with all the basic tools such as scissors, rulers, pencils, etc. on hand. Keep this area clean and have your decorating supplies well organized. This will go a long way to making efficient use of your time. In cooking, the French have a saying, mise en place – everything in its place. In practice what this means is that the chef gathers all the ingredients for the recipe, prepares them (cleans, cuts, measures, etc.) and puts them in small containers so everything is ready and on hand for the actual preparation. If you follow this technique, your card-making will be more fun and go quicker.

As you work, save your paper scraps. You will generate quite a lot of them, and scraps are ideal for making gift enclosures, tags, and bookmarks. All sizes and shapes are acceptable, since these items don't have to meet minimum postal sizes.

Making Cards

Your card design and the materials you include will dictate the order of assembly. The card projects in this book include step-by-step instructions to guide you and a list of the supplies you'll need. Although not listed with each project, some basic tools – ruler, scissors, bone folder, craft knife, light box – are used for almost every project.

Size of Cards

The first thing to decide is size. Cards can be any size you like, but there are mailing and paper stock considerations. Current U.S. postal rules state that a piece can be no smaller than 3-1/2" x 5" for mailing. A card of any size, if it's square, requires additional postage, regardless of weight. Many papers are 8-1/2" x 11" and, for economy, the size of the paper stock may dictate the card's size.

Finished sizes (open and folded, if applicable) are given for each card in this book. The **open size** is just that, the overall size when the card is completely opened up; the foundation paper will need to be large enough to accommodate those dimensions. The **folded size** is a guide for how large the envelope will need to be. Remember to add at least 1/4" to both dimensions for the envelope base, and more if the card is thick or bulky.

Measuring & Cutting

Careful measuring and cutting are the first steps. The old saw, "measure twice, cut once," holds true in card-making. A quilter's grid ruler is a real timesaver, but if you don't have one, use a metal ruler.

- **Straight cuts:** Mark either side of the sheet to be cut. Align the ruler and, holding it firmly with your fingers well out of the cutting path, draw the sharp, new blade of a craft knife along the edge.
- **Decorative Edges:** If you want a decorative edge, lightly draw a cutting guideline with a pencil and use an edger-type scissors to carefully cut along the line. Reposition the edger carefully and often to maintain a uniform cutting pattern.
- **Torn Edges:** Sometimes you'll want a torn edge on your paper. Tear slowly to keep the path under control. With difficult papers, use a paintbrush and water to loosen up a path to tear along-just paint on the water where you want to tear, then rip.

Folding

Mark and score first, then fold. Some papers fold more cleanly if the score is inside the fold; others if the score is to the outside. Test your paper to see which works best.

1. Score with the tip of a bone folder, a stylus, or very lightly with the tip of a craft knife, taking as much care to score the line straight as you would if you were cutting it.
2. Fold the paper.
3. With the bone folder, press a good, sharp crease along the fold.

Gluing

I like to use the least messy, least bulky, and quickest drying adhesive my work will allow. This varies from one card to the next, depending on the materials and techniques I'm using.

Technically, all my cards are collages, or assemblies, with a few exceptions. Generally, I'll create all the components of a card separately, if possible, and then assemble them from the base up. Sometimes a technique must be done directly on the card itself. Always test the technique and materials you're using before working on the actual card.

To glue paper to paper, consider the porosity or slickness of both surfaces. My first choice is a **glue pen**, but some papers are too porous and the glue is too wet – it soaks right into the paper and provides hardly any tack. Try the pen first and let dry. If it doesn't hold, re-glue with a different adhesive.

Glue sticks are another good choice for paper to paper situations. I find them a bit messier and harder to control than the pens, but they will cover a large area more quickly. Glue stick glue dries pretty fast, so you won't have a lot of time to reposition the components. Both glue pens and glue stick adhesives are fairly tidy to use – something to consider if you will later need to cut through the layered papers.

Dry, double-sided adhesives are faster to use than wet glues. The most basic of these is **double-sided tape** in a hand-held, disposable dispenser, and it will suffice in many situations. It doesn't make a good bond with all papers, especially those that are heavier and have slick or coated surfaces. It may work fine for a single layer, but if you then add more layers, putting more stress on the base layers, the tape may pull loose. Special "strong bond" tapes (read the package information) will work in most instances where ordinary tape won't hold.

Double-sided sheet adhesives take more time to apply than liquid glue or glue sticks – you have to cut to shape, then peel off liner paper from both sides of the adhesive – and they are bulkier

1. Scoring with a bone folder.

2. Creasing with a bone folder.

and more difficult to cut through in successive steps. Double-sided adhesive sheets are available in permanent or repositionable. When a sturdy bond is needed, permanent is preferred.

For collage work, especially that involving glass or metal objects, use a **jeweler's glue or specialty glue** recommended for these materials. Allow the glue to dry thoroughly before proceeding; the glue can leave residue where you don't want it if you happen to bump the card and move the object before the glue has had a chance to set up.

Card Liners

Paper can be inserted into your cards for writing a personal message. Stationery weight paper is the best choice. Cut the liner a little smaller than the size of the opened card. The liner can be left loose, can be attached to the card fold with glue or tied with ribbon, or it can be glued to one open side of the card if you wish to hide the backside of something. When attaching liners to cards, glue the liner to one half of the folded card only! If you glue the liner paper to both halves of the folded card, the card will not fold properly.

Making Envelopes

It may be necessary to create an envelope for your card. To do that, start with a flat panel slightly larger than the card itself and add four flaps that will fold to surround the card. If you don't have a single sheet of paper large enough to accomplish this, you can attach separate pieces for the flaps.

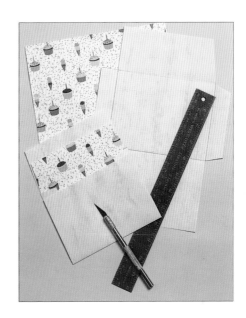

- *Vellum envelopes are a special way to let everyone who handles the card get a glimpse of the wonderful treasure that lies within.*
- *Cards with bulky collages may require a padded outer envelope to protect them on their journey through the mail. But for an elegant presentation, first enclose your creation in an envelope that is as attractive as the card itself.*
- *Envelope liners will set an ordinary envelope apart from the rest. Add them to your handmade envelopes and to ones that you buy.*
- *Any paper can be used for envelopes, but the U.S. Postal Service may add a printed bar code or bar code sticker along the bottom edge, so keep that in mind as you design. If you are decorating plain paper, leave a clean 1/2" margin along the bottom edge for postal use.*
- *Test the adhesive you plan to use to be sure it will hold the paper you've selected.*

Supplies

Paper, Ruler, Scissors or craft knife, Adhesive of your choice

Basic Method

1. **Determine the size of the envelope.** Add 1/4" to 1/2" to width and height of card to provide the dimensions for the envelope front. Double the height and add at least 1/2" for a top flap. Add 1/2" to 1" to each side for flaps. The back can be slightly shorter than the front, so subtract 1/4" to 1/2" from the overall height and add it to the top flap.
2. *Piece the paper, if necessary.* Piece the flaps, being sure to add paper for overlapping, on the base panel if you can't get the whole envelope out of one sheet of paper. If you are piecing, consider making the top flap from a contrasting or complementary paper. The edge of the top flap can be trimmed with decorative scissors or cut into an unusual shape. (See Fig. 1) Cut the side flaps at the top and bottom at slight angles to ensure a nice fit when they are folded and glued into place.
3. **Cut.** Cut out the shape. (See Fig. 2)
4. **Score.** Score along the fold lines. (See Fig. 3)
5. **Fold.** Lay the envelope face down, with the outside front to your work surface. Fold the side flaps toward the inside of the envelope.

Add an envelope liner at this point, if desired. (See Fig. 4)
6. **Glue.** Apply adhesive to the side flaps. Fold the back panel up and affix to the glue.
7. **Insert the card.** Place the card in the envelope and secure the top flap in place, taking care not to get any adhesive on the card inside.

Liners

It's easy to add a liner to an envelope. See Figs. 5 and 6 on page 39.
On a handmade envelope:
1. **Cut.** Cut the liner to fit below your final glue strip and just slightly smaller than the width of the card. The liner can extend all the way into the envelope to the bottom fold. It should end at least 1-1/2" from the top fold.
2. **Glue.** Apply adhesive to the top edge of the liner only, and affix the liner to envelope before you glue the envelope back to the side flaps.

On a purchased envelope:
1. **Cut.** Trace around the opened envelope flap and sides on the chosen liner paper. Trim the paper so it will fit below the glue strip and inside the envelope at least 1-1/2" below the fold.
2. **Glue.** Apply adhesive to the top edge only of the liner and insert into envelope.

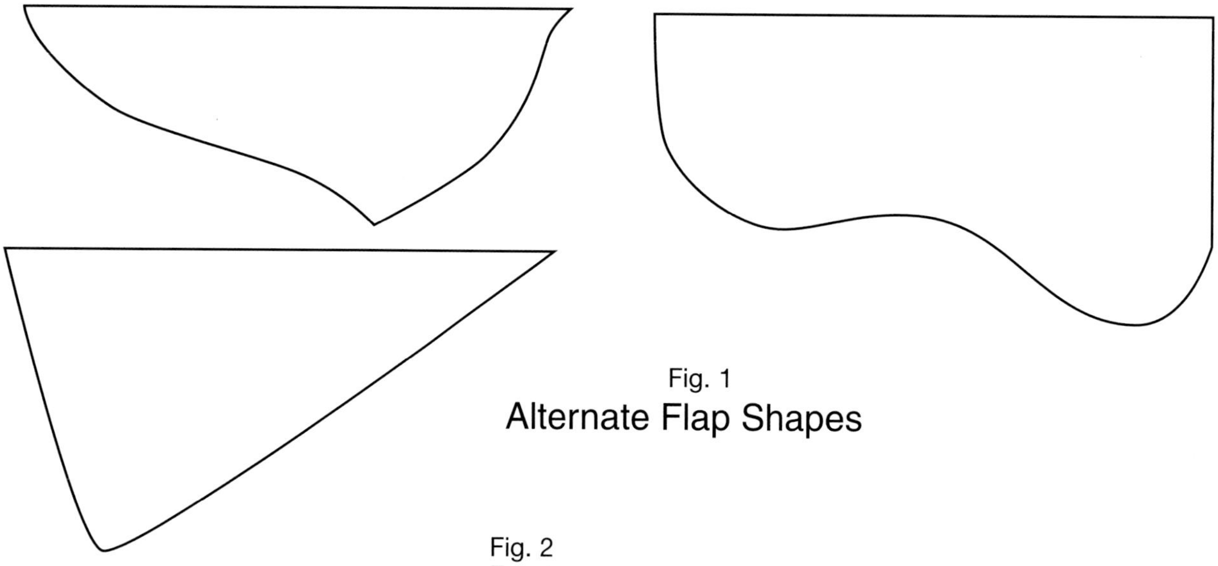

Fig. 1
Alternate Flap Shapes

Fig. 2
Envelope
pattern

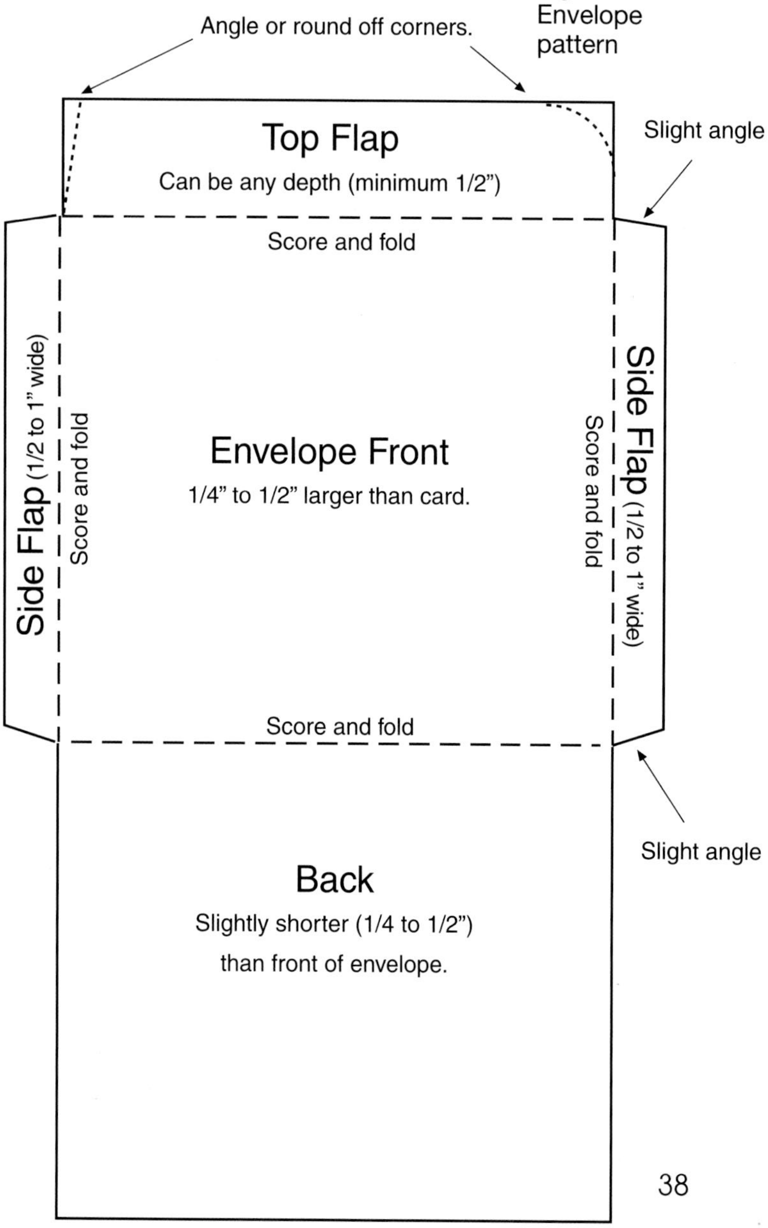

Angle or round off corners.

Slight angle

Top Flap
Can be any depth (minimum 1/2")

Score and fold

Side Flap (1/2 to 1" wide)

Score and fold

Envelope Front
1/4" to 1/2" larger than card.

Side Flap (1/2 to 1" wide)

Score and fold

Score and fold

Slight angle

Back
Slightly shorter (1/4 to 1/2")
than front of envelope.

Fig. 3
Folding
the side
flaps

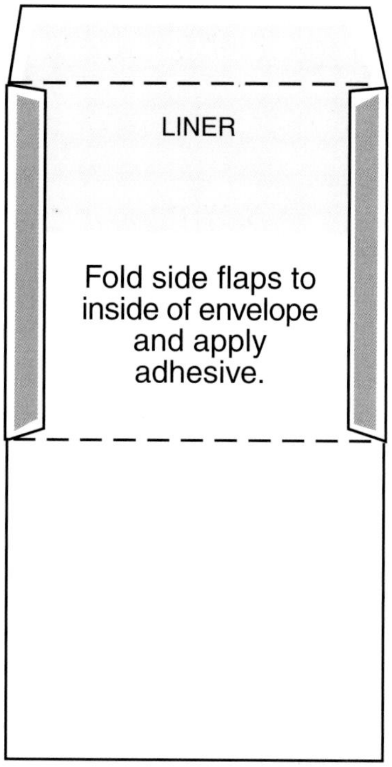

LINER

Fold side flaps to
inside of envelope
and apply
adhesive.

Fig. 4
Folding
the back
panel

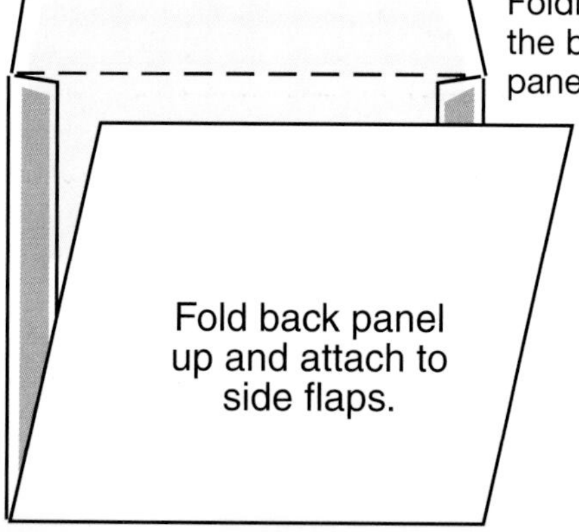

Fold back panel
up and attach to
side flaps.

38

Add liner to handmade envelope before gluing.

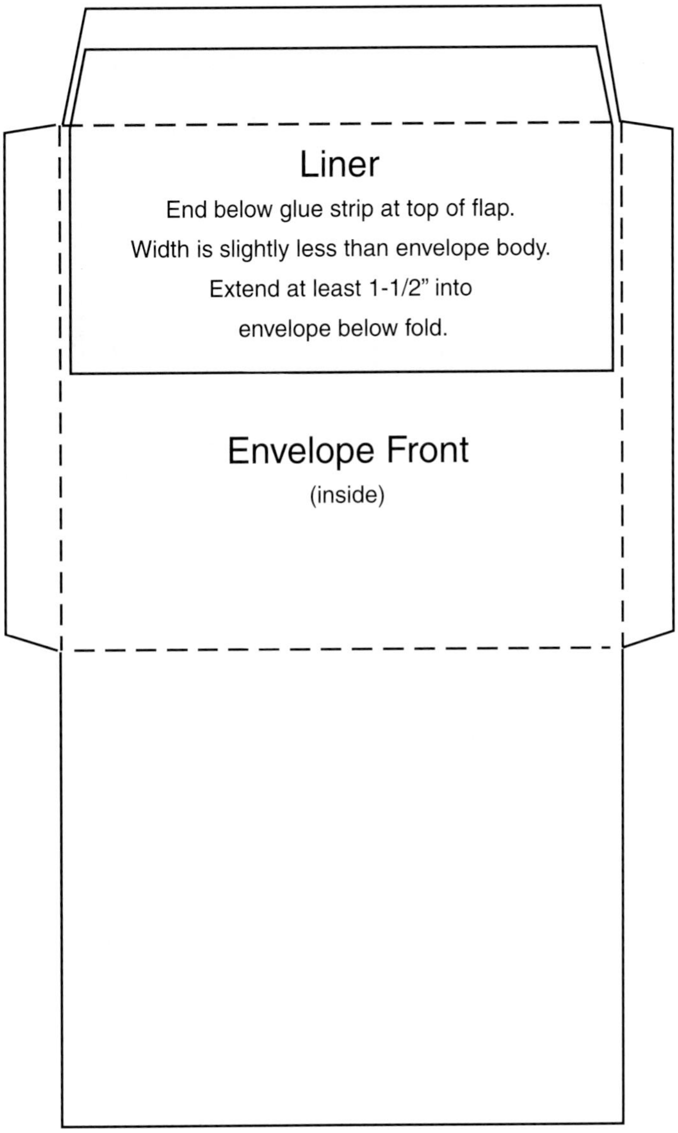

Liner

End below glue strip at top of flap.

Width is slightly less than envelope body.

Extend at least 1-1/2" into

envelope below fold.

Envelope Front

(inside)

Fig. 5
Adding a liner to a handmade envelope.

How to add a liner to a pre-made envelope.

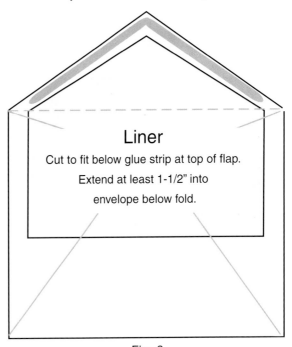

Liner

Cut to fit below glue strip at top of flap.

Extend at least 1-1/2" into

envelope below fold.

Fig. 6
Adding a liner to a purchased envelope.

Any Occasion Cards

Whether you wish to say "I miss you," or "You are Special," or "Thank You," this chapter is the place to find an appropriate design. The cards in this chapter are adaptable to any occasion — just add an appropriate message.

Pictured clockwise, starting at top right: Language of Flowers, Life's Blessings, Thank You for Dinner, Gazebo, All Tied Up

Of all life's blessings,
you are the best.

Thank you so much!

Thank You for Dinner

Pictured on page 41

I found the miniature silverware in a doll set at a shop that sells gifts and antiques.
If you can't find something similar, consider using stamps or clip art for the utensils.

Open size: 6" x 9"

Folded size: 6" x 4-1/2"

Techniques: ♥

Supplies

Papers:

Purchased card and envelope, spice colors

Image of food, 2-5/8" wide x 3-3/8" tall (from wrapping paper or a magazine)

Card stock, off white

Paper printed with clouds, off white (for envelope liner)

Decorative Elements:

Miniature metal fork and knife

Rubber stamp for message ("Thank you so much!")

Embossing ink

Silver embossing powder

Tools & Other Supplies:

Stencil for embossing frames

Paper-edgers, Victorian

Embossing heat tool

Needle tool

Double-sided foam carpet tape

Glue stick or glue pen

Jeweler's glue

Step-by-Step

1. Stamp the message on scrap paper. Measure the width and height of the stamped message. Cut a window in the front of the card slightly larger than the message.

2. Using the straight edge of any lightweight stencil, stencil-emboss a frame around the window.

3. Stamp the message inside the card, positioning the stamp so the message shows through the window. Emboss with silver powder.

4. Mark a 3-1/4" x 4" rectangle on off-white card stock. Trim with Victorian edgers. Stencil-emboss a simple rectangle frame to outline the food image. Paper-prick around the edges, following the design made by the edgers. Attach the image to the off white frame with a glue stick or glue pen.

5. For added dimension, use foam carpet tape to attach the framed image to the front of the card.

6. Attach the miniature silverware with jeweler's glue.

7. Use edgers to shape the edge of the envelope flap and to trim a liner for the envelope from off white cloud paper. Paper-prick the edges of the liner before attaching it to the envelope. ❑

All Tied Up

Pictured on page 41

The beautiful embossed papers make this card unique. It would be particularly suitable for Valentine's Day or a birthday.

Open size: 8-3/4" x 6"

Folded size: 4-3/8" x 6"

Techniques:

Supplies

Paper:

Blank card and envelope, white

Leather look embossed paper, olive, 4-3/8" x 6"

Leather look embossed paper - blue, 3-1/4" x 5"

Leather look embossed paper - cream, 2" x 3-1/2"

Striped liner paper, cream and silver

Decorative Elements:

Sheer ribbon, 1" wide, one piece 24" long, another 18" long

Rubber stamp (text of poem "How Do I Love Thee?")

Embossing ink

Embossing powder, gold

Tools & Other Supplies:

Embossing heat tool

Double-sided adhesive

Step-by Step

1. Dip the edges of the cream embossed paper in embossing ink, then in embossing powder. Apply heat to emboss.

2. Stack and affix to the card front the olive panel, then the blue panel, and finally the cream panel. Center each and use double-sided adhesive to attach.

3. Tie the 24" length of ribbon around longer dimension of card front and knot. Tie the shorter ribbon around the shorter dimension and knot around first knot. Trim the ribbon ends with inverted V-notches to finish.

4. Fold the striped liner paper in half. Stamp and emboss the poem on the top half.

5. Use double-sided adhesive to attach to the inside of the card front. ❏

Life's Blessings

Pictured on page 41

This would be great as a birthday or Mother's Day card or to express your appreciation for a meaningful relationship. The message I used was torn from a parchment sheet of printed sentiments commercially available for decoupage.

Open size: 10-1/4" x 7"

Folded size: 5-1/2" x 7"

Techniques:

Supplies

Paper:

Printed card stock, leaf design in golds on one side, off white on the other, 10-1/4" x 7"

Vellum, pastel gold, 5-3/4" x 7"

Card stock, off white, 3-1/2" x 2-3/4"

Torn parchment paper with printed message

Feather motifs cut from wrapping paper

Decorative Elements:

Rubber stamps, feather images

Embossing ink

Embossing powders - gold, pearlized, lavender

Metal embossing stencil, border designs

Tools & Other Supplies:

Glue pen

Glue stick

Step-by-Step

1. Score the leaf-printed paper 4-3/4" from one end. Fold with leaves to outside. Note the 3/4" wide exposed off-white margin.

2. Open up the card. Stamp and emboss feather images, one at a time, along the margin, letting the images bleed off the edges. Alternate gold, pearlized, and lavender embossing powders. (Be sure to protect your work surface with scrap paper).

3. Score a flap in the vellum 1" from one short end. Stamp feathers with embossing ink all over the large panel, again letting the images bleed off the edge. Emboss with pearlized powder. (Since you are using just one powder color for this step, you can do all the stamping and embossing together.)

4. Apply adhesive to the flap of the vellum, align the vellum and card at the folds, and attach the vellum flap to the back of the card.

5. Stencil-emboss a decorative border on the off white card stock.

6. Glue the torn parchment message and feather motif on the stencil-embossed paper. Attach this assembly to the front of the card.

7. Glue an additional feather motif to the card front. ❏

Gazebo

Pictured on page 41

A calendar and a gardening supply catalog were the sources for the images on this card. A layer of vellum on the outside of the card mutes the color image cut from a calendar. A garden scene cut from a catalog shows through the opening on the front of the card.

Open size: 11" x 7"

Folded size: 5-1/2" x 7"

Techniques: ❑

Supplies

Paper:

Card stock, pastel, 11" x 7"

Vellum, 7" x 7"

Laser-cut paper gazebo

Image for cover, 7" x 7" (garden scene cut from a calendar)

Image for inside, 3-3/4" x 4-1/2" (garden scene cut from a catalog)

Decorative Elements:

Small metal garland, grapes motif

Tools & Other Supplies:

Thin cardboard for making a template

Glue pen

Glue stick

Double-sided adhesive

Jeweler's glue

Toothpick

Wax paper

Book or other weight

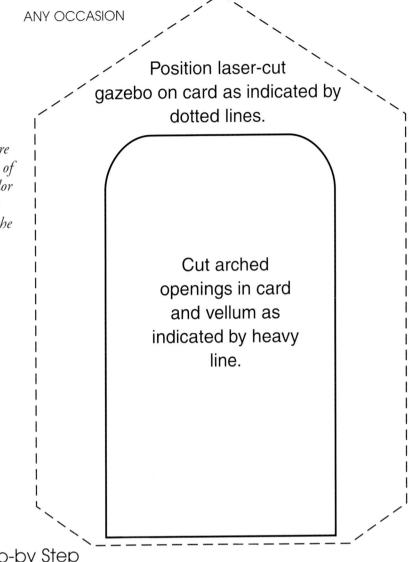

Position laser-cut gazebo on card as indicated by dotted lines.

Cut arched openings in card and vellum as indicated by heavy line.

Step-by Step

1. Cut a template for the window, using the pattern provided.

2. Score the card stock and fold in half.

3. Attach the cover color image (garden scene cut from a calendar) to the card front, using a glue stick or double-sided adhesive.

4. Use the template to mark the window opening in the card front. Cut out.

5. Attach the smaller image to the inside of the card so it shows through the window.

6. Score and fold a 1-1/2" flap in the vellum. Attach vellum flap to back of card, with folds aligned.

7. Mark and cut window in vellum to match the one in the card front.

8. Center the laser-cut gazebo on the vellum cover and attach, using a glue pen.

9. Bend the metal garland to fit around the gazebo doorway and trim to fit.

10. Use jeweler's glue, applied in small amounts with a toothpick to the back of the garland, to adhere the garland to the gazebo. Cover with wax paper and weight with a book until dry. ❑

Language of Flowers

Pictured on page 41

This card keeps unfolding randomly to reveal beautiful pictures of flowers and their meaning. Because the botanical paper I used for the foundation of the card is very porous and textured, I knew it would be difficult to write my messages directly on it. That's why I chose to make a background with complementary paper for each flower motif. If your foundation paper is more conducive to writing, you could omit the backgrounds.

Open size: 17-3/4" wide x 18-1/2" tall

Folded size: 5" x 5"

Techniques: ❑

Supplies

Paper:

Botanical handmade paper, 18" x 19" for foundation of card

Decorative embossed and highlighted paper, 6" x 6" for front decorative panel

Vellum, pastel green, 4" x 4-1/4" for writing sentiment

Flower motifs cut from gardening catalogs and trimmed to fit on panels indicated on pattern (11 in all)

Additional vellum or solid papers for backgrounds on which flowers will be glued

Decorative Elements:

Fine-tip markers, various colors

Small stickers, flower motifs

Paint pen, gold metallic

Other Tools & Supplies:

Micro-tip scissors

Glue stick

Step-by-Step

1. Cut out botanical paper, using pattern provided.

2. Score and fold the botanical paper as indicated on the pattern.

3. Tear embossed and highlighted paper to a size slightly smaller than the front cover panel.

4. Carefully tear out a heart shape from the center of the embossed and highlighted paper, using pattern provided. Edge the heart opening with gold metallic paint pen. Attach heart panel to front of card.

5. Glue the trimmed images of flowers to vellum or pastel paper. Write a message or sentiment with fine marker close to the flower image. Trim the background paper close to the image and glue to the appropriate panel. NOTE: Be sure to fold and open the card before affixing images to panels; some images need to be applied upside down, so they will be correctly oriented as the recipient unfolds the card.

6. On the green vellum, use a marker to write the message shown in the illustration on next page. Use a grid or lined paper beneath as a guide to keep the baselines straight.

7. Use small flower stickers to hold the vellum to the botanical paper. Reinforce with a sturdier adhesive and hide it with the stickers, if necessary. ❑

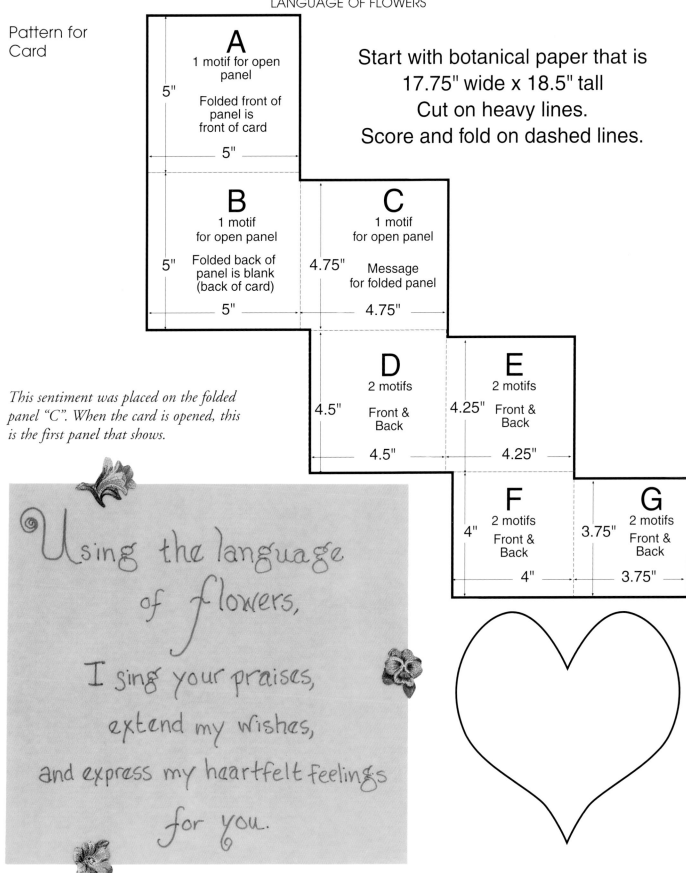

Pattern for
Card

A
1 motif for open panel

Folded front of panel is front of card

5"

5"

B
1 motif for open panel

Folded back of panel is blank (back of card)

5"

5"

C
1 motif for open panel

Message for folded panel

4.75"

4.75"

Start with botanical paper that is
17.75" wide x 18.5" tall
Cut on heavy lines.
Score and fold on dashed lines.

This sentiment was placed on the folded panel "C". When the card is opened, this is the first panel that shows.

D
2 motifs

Front & Back

4.5"

4.5"

E
2 motifs

Front & Back

4.25"

4.25"

F
2 motifs

Front & Back

4"

4"

G
2 motifs

Front & Back

3.75"

3.75"

Using the language
of flowers,

I sing your praises,

extend my wishes,

and express my heartfelt feelings

for you.

47

Triangle Notes

These will fit in a standard #10 business envelope. Since you can make one card so quickly, consider doing several at a time so you'll always have one on hand. I used two paint colors on each card. To make the process faster, especially if you are doing several cards, cut a sponge triangle for each paint color you are using.

Open size: 7-1/2" x 8-1/2"

Folded size: 3-3/4" x 8-1/2"

Techniques: ❏ ✳ ❈

Supplies

Paper:
Card stock for foundations
Papers for backgrounds

Decorative Elements:
Acrylic metallic paint in coordinating colors
Compressed sponge
Metal leaf and leaf adhesive

Tools & Other Supplies:
Adhesive
Wax paper or palette

Pattern for triangle motif

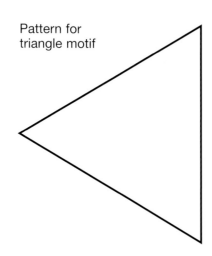

Step-by-Step

1. Trim and score card stock for the foundation.
2. Select a paper for the decorative background.
3. Cut a triangle shape out of compressed sponge, using the pattern provided. Dip in water to expand. Squeeze out excess water.
4. Squeeze a puddle of paint on a piece of wax paper or other palette.

48

5. Dip the sponge in the paint to load it. Test on a scrap of paper. Stamp a row of triangles on the paper background, using photo as a guide for placement. Let dry.
6. Cut a 1" square piece of sponge. Dip in water to expand. Squeeze out excess water. Use the sponge to apply metal leaf adhesive on the triangle-stamped paper.
7. Apply the leaf to the adhesive squares.
8. Trim the stamped paper to fit the front of the card. Affix with double-sided adhesive or glue stick. Vary the angles and combine with other papers for added visual interest. ❏

Pictured, top to bottom: Sorry, Sun & Moon, Retro Cafe

Sun & Moon

This flat card carries a petite card that opens by folding back the sun and moon, then lifting the flap to reveal the message.

Size: 8-1/2" x 5-1/2"

Techniques:

Supplies

Paper:

Stardust paper, lavender, 8-1/2" x 5-1/2" for foundation of card

Stardust paper, lilac and silver, small scraps for punched images

Velveteen paper, purple, 8-1/2" x 5-1/2" for layered front panel

Two-tone paper, lilac/deep lilac, 3" x 5" for small message card

Cover stock, cream, 2-1/2" x 3" for moon

Cover stock, yellow, 2-1/2" x 3" for sun

Decorative Elements:

Paper embossing stencils with sun and moon motifs

Rubber stamps appropriate to your message

Stamp pad, purple

Gel pen, black

Tools & Other Supplies:

Punches - spiral, star, tiny moon

Paper edgers, wave

Glue stick

Glue pen

Double-sided adhesive

Micro-tip scissors

Step-by-Step

1. Cut foundation card from lavender stardust paper.

2. Apply double-sided adhesive to the back of the velveteen paper. Trim all sides with wave edger to 5" x 8".

3. Punch stars and moons out of the velveteen paper. (Most punches will not reach into the center of the paper, so just punch around the edges and as far into the panel as you can.)

4. Center the velveteen panel on the lavender stardust panel. Attach.

5. Score and fold the two-tone paper to 3" x 2-1/2" to create the small card. Hand write a message inside this card and decorate it with a stamped image if desired.

6. Paper-emboss a moon on the cream cover stock and a sun on the yellow cover stock. Carefully trim out parts of the images, leaving enough to score and fold a flap on the left side of the moon and the right side of the sun. See Fig. 1.

7. Attach the flaps of the sun and moon to the back of the little lilac card.

8. Use double-sided adhesive to attach the lilac card to the front of the velveteen panel.

9. Punch spirals from small scraps of lilac and silver stardust. Use a glue pen to apply adhesive to the backs of the punched stars and spirals. Glue stars and spirals to the velveteen panel.

10. Carefully intertwine the sun rays with the moon motif to hold the little card closed. ❏

Fig. 1 - Scoring guide for insert

score   score

Retro Cafe

Pictured on page 50

You can adapt this card for many different occasions – a birthday, "let's meet," "thanks for lunch," or "I miss you" are just a few of the possibilities. The handmade envelope is lined with a checkerboard paper.

Open size: 9" x 6"

Folded size: 4-1/2" x 6"

Techniques:

Supplies

Paper:

Purchased card and envelope, hot pink

Card stock, white

Card stock, pink

Tissue paper to use for design/pattern placement

Stardust papers - black, pink, magenta, and pink diamond pattern

Vellum with black checks, for envelope liner

Decorative Elements:

Rubber stamp with chair and table motif

Stamp pad with black ink

Tools & Other Supplies:

Spiral punch

See-through ruler with 1/4" grid

Double-sided adhesive

Glue pen

Glue stick

Step-by-Step

1. Cut a large trapezoid and small triangle shape from black stardust paper. Cut a triangle shape from pink diamond stardust.

2. Stamp the image on white card stock, pink card stock, and tissue paper. Mark a frame around one of the card stock images with pencil. (This one is a 3-1/4" square.) Overlay the tissue image, and mark the frame on the tissue to match. Use the tissue image to mark an identical frame on the second card stock image. Trim both images along frame lines.

3. Use one of the trimmed images with the background components to arrange the collage. Attach the background shapes to the card front.

4. Cut a piece of double-sided adhesive slightly smaller than a trimmed, stamped image. Do not remove the paper liner yet. Carefully slice the stamped image on the pink card stock and the stamped image on the white card stock into 1/4" vertical strips. Start cutting from the same edge of both images, and use the grid of the ruler to get even, uniform cuts. The goal is to have the same portion of the stamped image on each of two colored strips.

5. Remove the paper liner from one side of the double-side adhesive shape. To it, apply alternating strips of the card stock to re-create the stamped image in pink and white stripes.

6. Peel off the second liner paper and apply the striped image to the card.

7. Punch spirals from black, pink, and magenta stardust paper. Use the glue pen to apply adhesive to the backs of punched designs. Affix each to the card.

8. Line the envelope with black checked vellum. ❏

Sorry...

Pictured on page 50

Finding just the right image of a regretful person is the key to this card. I found mine in a clip art book.

Open size: 8-1/2" x 11"

Folded size: 8-1/2" x 5-1/2"

Techniques: ✳ ☐ ♥

Supplies

Paper:

Handmade marbled paper, fuchsia, 8-1/2" x 5-1/2" for card front panel

Card stock, cream, 8-1/2" x 11" for card foundation

Wavy corrugated paper, white, small strip

Clip art image of woman copied on cream paper

Decorative Elements:

Stickers for inside of card

Stencil for message

Colored pencils

Stamp pad, magenta

Gold foil and foil adhesive

Tools & Other Supplies:

Oval template, 5" x 3-1/2"

Glue stick

Double-sided adhesive

Step-by-Step

1. Lightly color the clip art with colored pencils. Cut out image.

2. Score and fold the cream card stock in half.

3. Position the trimmed clip art image on the inside right panel and adhere with a glue stick.

4. Place the oval template over the image for the appropriate position to make a window in the front of the card. Carefully close the card. Without moving the template, turn the card and template over, and lay on your work surface. Open the card and trace the oval on the inside front panel of the card.

5. Use a stencil with a fuchsia colored pencil to create the lettering around the oval shape on the inside of card, "I've had a lot on my mind."

6. Position stickers above the clip art image.

7. Adhere the fuchsia marble paper to the front of the card, using a good coating of glue from the glue stick. Let dry.

8. Carefully cut the oval opening through both layers of the card front.

9. Close the card and stencil the lettering on the front with a dark gray pencil, leaving plenty of clearance near the bottom for the small chips that frame the oval.

10. To make the "mosaic" chips, lightly rub a small piece of corrugated paper over the surface of a magenta stamp pad. Let dry. Brush the corrugated paper with foil adhesive. Let dry until tacky. Apply the foil.

11. Apply double-sided adhesive to the back of the corrugated paper. Cut into 1/2" strips. Cut the strips into small squares. Affix the squares around the lower half of the oval, using photo as a guide. ❑

Beaded Butterflies

These beautiful beaded butterflies will make any card special. The butterflies can be glued onto the card; or pinbacks can be glued to the back of the butterflies then the butterflies pinned to the card. The recipient of the card can then wear the butterfly as a pin. The supply listing and instructions are for creating the card on this page that has four butterflies. For a simpler card, you can use one or two butterflies to decorate purchased blank cards as shown in the photo on page 55.

Open size: 8-1/2" x 11"

Folded size: 8-1/2" x 5-1/2"

Techniques: ○

Supplies

Paper:

Card stock, green gingham print, 8-1/2" x 11" for card foundation

Card stock, vellum, 8-1/2" x 11", two sheets

Card stock, lavender, 8-1/2" x 11" for making butterflies

Decorative Elements:

Stencil with butterfly designs

Metallic acrylic craft paint - blue, periwinkle, amethyst, rose, plum, peridot, teal, emerald

4 flower beads and mauve bugle beads for border

Assorted seed and bugle beads for butterflies

Frosted small cabochon

Ellipse bead

Glitter paint with small applicator tip, purple

Tools & Other Supplies:

Dimensional adhesive dots

Stencil brushes or sponges

Fine gauge wire, about 5"

Needle tool

Glue stick

Double-sided adhesive

Micro-tip scissors

Step-by-Step

1. Fold gingham print card stock to 5-1/2" x 8-1/2".

2. Fold vellum card stock to same size as gingham card. Insert gingham card into vellum card. Attach the vellum cover to the card with double-sided adhesive along the back spine.

3. On front of vellum, apply flower and bugle beads to make a border, using purple glitter paint as a glue. See photo for placement. Set aside to dry.

4. Stencil butterfly motifs in colors of your choice on both the lavender and vellum card stocks. Let dry.

5. Cut out the shapes from the lavender stock. Set aside.

6. Cut out the vellum butterflies and remove the antennae.

7. To decorate the bodies and wings with beads, apply a short strip of glitter paint, pick up several beads on the end of a piece of wire, and carefully slide the beads off the wire into the paint. Use the needle tool to push them into position. Work in small areas, giving yourself enough time to arrange the beads before the paint starts to set up. Let each butterfly dry completely before handling.

8. Arrange the lavender stock (base) butterflies on the card front. Attach with glue or double-sided adhesive.

9. Cut dimensional adhesive dots to fit the butterfly bodies and apply to the base butterflies. Use the "waste" material surrounding the dots on small areas.

10. Attach the vellum beaded butterflies to the base shapes on top of the adhesive dot pieces. ❏

Silk Beaded Heart

Open size: 7" x 10"

Folded size: 7" x 5"

Techniques: ○ ◻ 🔨

Supplies

Paper:

Card stock, lavender, 7" x 10" for base

Card stock, lilac, for inside message

Wavy corrugated paper, white, 7" x 5" for front panel

Decorative Elements:

5" x 7" swatch of 100% silk fabric

Silk dyes - purple, emerald, blue

Marking pens - purple, magenta, green

Upholstery braid with 1/2" flange, blue and white

Seed beads - purple (two sizes), blue

Bugle beads, mauve

Decorative flower bead, mauve

Small shank button, silver

Rubber stamps with heart motifs

Tools & Other Supplies:

Beading thread and needle

Small amount of batting

Small sharp needle and sewing thread

Blank sticker paper

Tape

Double-sided adhesive

Step-by-Step

1. Following the basic method in the techniques section, paint the silk with the dyes. Set aside to dry.
2. Decorate the painted silk with markers. Let dry.
3. Score and fold the lavender card stock to 5" x 7".
4. Apply a message using your choice of technique on the lilac card stock.

5. Tear around the message in a heart shape that fits within the 5" x 7" area.
6. Trace the heart pattern on the back side of the corrugated paper. Cut out an opening with a craft knife.
7. Use double-sided tape to apply the flange of the upholstery trim to the back of the corrugated card around the heart opening. Snip the flange to curve as necessary.
8. Using beading thread and needle anchored to back of upholstery trim, starting at the bottom, string on a blue seed bead, 5 small purple seeds, a large purple seed, a bugle, a blue seed, and a small purple seed. Take needle back through blue, bugle, and large purple seed. String on 5 more small purple and one blue seed. Stitch through trim approximately 3/8" from start. Bring needle back through blue and one small purple seed. Add four more small purple seeds and repeat sequence, working all the way around the heart shape.
9. At the end, make a small tassel by stringing through the flower bead, add a few seeds and/or a bugle, go back through the flower bead, and make a stitch into the trim. Go back through the flower and string on more beads for another strand of the tassel. Make three strands extending from the flower bead.
10. To keep the beaded fringe in place, tack some of the fringe ends with small invisible stitches to the card using sewing needle and beading thread.

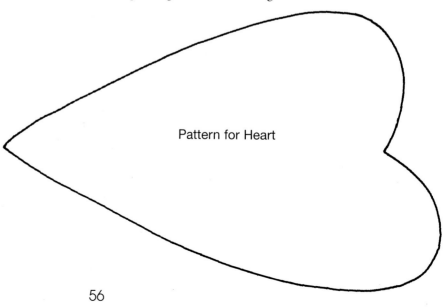

Pattern for Heart

11. Tape the painted silk to the back of the panel, allowing some slack to accommodate the batting. Shape the batting and place at the center of the silk.

12. Apply double-sided adhesive to the outside front of the lavender card. Apply the corrugated panel, with silk and batting in place, aligning with fold, to the front of the card.

13. Sew the button to the middle of the heart with sewing needle and thread. Tie a secure knot on the inside of the card.

14. Use a heart stamp to make a small sticker on blank sticker paper to cover the thread knot.

15. Attach the torn heart-shaped message to the inside of the card. ❑

Best Wishes

Size: 5-1/2" x 4-1/4"

Techniques: ☐

Supplies:

Paper:

Card stock, purple, 5-1/2" x 8-1/2" for base card

Card stock, ecru, 3" x 4" for message

Metallic gold crinkled paper, 3-1/2" x 4-1/2" for layer behind greeting

Decorative Elements:

Stencil with words "Best Wishes"

Metal embossing stencil with border design

Stencil paint, gold

Gel pen, gold

Tools & Other Supplies:

Embossing tool

Stencil brush

Glue stick

Step-by-Step

1. Emboss the ecru card with the border design.

2. Measure, mark, and emboss a rectangle in the center of this piece just larger than the stencil design.

3. Stencil words in center of ecru piece with gold paint.

4. Use the same stencil brush and paint to pounce gold around the edge of the purple card stock.

5. Score and crease purple card stock to create a folded card.

6. Glue stenciled piece to gold liner piece to create a border.

7. Glue both to front of purple card. Center side to side and place 1/8" down from fold at top.

8. Write message inside with a gold pen. ❏

Sweet Pea

Size: 5-1/2" x 4-1/4"

Techniques:

Supplies

Paper:

Card stock, ecru, 5-1/2" x 8-1/2" for base card

Parchment paper, 5-1/2" x 8-1/2"

Decorative Elements:

Stencil with sweet pea motif

Metal embossing stencil with words and flowers

Stencil paints - rose, burgundy, light green, medium green

Sheer white ribbon, 1/4" wide, 10" long

Tools & Other Supplies:

Embossing tool

Stencil brush

Hole punch

Step-by-Step

1. Score and crease card stock and parchment at center to create folded cards.

2. Emboss entire piece of parchment with random words and flowers.

3. Stencil a flower on the front of the ecru card stock with rose paint. Shade with burgundy. Stencil the leaves with light green. Shade with medium green. Allow to dry.

4. Insert stenciled card inside parchment. Measure and mark for two punched holes 1" apart to accommodate ribbon. Punch holes and tie the card together with the ribbon. ❏

Bright Greetings

These cards are quick and easy to make. Using colored markers for stenciling is fun, and there are no brushes to clean up afterwards. Because markers sometimes bleed under a stencil, I lightly "scribbled" the marker over the stencil opening, working in the same direction for all the letters. Having gaps in the marker lines adds to the casual, fun look.

Both cards are done with the same technique – only the paper color is different.

Size: 8-1/2" x 4-1/2"

Techniques:

Supplies

Paper:

Embossed card stock, 8-1/2" x 9" for card base

Card stock, white, 8-1/2" x 4-1/2" for stenciling

Colored paper, 8-1/2" x 4-1/2" for middle layer under stenciled piece

Corrugated paper scrap (used on "Celebrate" card)

Writing paper, 8-1/2" x 9" for inside of card

Decorative Elements:

Stencil with letters and motifs

Colored markers

Tools & Other Supplies: Glue stick

Step-by-Step

1. Stencil design on white card stock, using markers in a variety of colors.
2. Cut white card stock closely around stenciling.
3. Cut a liner to make a border for the stenciled piece, cutting liner 1/2" larger than stenciled piece in both directions.
4. Glue stenciled piece to liner piece.
5. Score and crease embossed paper, folding in half.
6. Center stenciled piece on front of card and glue in place.
7. *Option:* On "Celebrate" card, scraps of corrugated paper were glued to each side of stencil piece to look like a ribbon.
8. Insert writing paper. ❑

Ivy & Dragonflies

Open size: 8-1/2" x 11"

Folded size: 8-1/2" x 5-1/2"

Techniques: ♥ ◎ ☐

Supplies

Card stock, light green parchment,
   8-1/2" x 11" folded to 8-1/2" x 5-1/2"
   for base card
Vellum
Printed paper, light green, 9" x 11-1/2"
   for card liner

Decorative Elements:
Stencils with ivy and dragonfly motifs
Acrylic metallic paints - peridot, emerald,
   lavender, plum, teal, blue
26 gauge wire - turquoise, purple

Tools & Other Supplies:
Stencil sponges or brushes
Micro-tip scissors
Round-nose pliers
Wire cutters
Glue gun and glue sticks
Glue stick

Step-by-Step

1. Fold and crease green parchment and printed paper.
2. Stencil ivy motifs on parchment card front using emerald and peridot. Let dry.
3. Use a craft knife with very sharp blade to cut around leaf tips. Carefully bend the cut leaf areas forward.
4. Stencil four dragonflies on vellum in colors of your choice. Stencil four additional dragonfly bodies on vellum. Let dry.
5. Cut out dragonflies and extra bodies. Glue the complete dragonflies to the card front.
6. Twist wire into simple antennae and tail shapes. Glue to dragonflies on card.
7. Apply hot glue to wired bodies on card, letting it remain slightly raised. Carefully position the additional bodies on top to cover the wires and add dimension.
8. Slip printed paper inside card, with printed side facing out. Secure front with a glue stick. (If the back of your printed paper is not white, you may need to add another insert for writing a message.) ❏

Simple Leaves

Open size: 8-1/2" x 11"

Folded size: 8-1/2" x 6"

Techniques:

Supplies

Paper:
Two-tone card stock, light sage/sage,
   8-1/2" x 11" folded to 8-1/2" x 6" with
   light color to front
Paper, sage, 5" x 7"

Decorative Elements:
Stencils with wavy edge and assorted leaf
   motifs
Acrylic metallic paint - gold, copper,
   champagne, peridot

8" twig
26 gauge copper wire

Tools & Other Supplies:
Stencil sponges or brushes
Micro-tip scissors
Wire cutters
Paper punch, 1/32" hole
Glue stick or glue pen

Step-by-Step

1. Stencil a wavy border using peridot along edge of card front. Let dry.
2. Mask the border with the same stencil. Stencil a leaf background using gold and copper mixed with champagne to make varying shades. Stencil lightest colored leaves first, then overlay with gradually darker colors.
3. Stencil two leaves in darker shades on separate piece of sage paper. Let dry. Cut out and slightly curl the edges.
4. Position the twig along the contrasting margin of the folded card. Mark six vertical positions along one side of the twig lightly with pencil. Remove the twig and mark corresponding positions 1/8" from the first six. Punch the 12 holes with tiny hole punch.
5. Lace the copper wire through the holes to secure the twig to the card, going back and forth several times.
6. Glue the cutout leaves to the front of the card. ❏

Photo Cards

Photo cards are a wonderful way to keep in touch with friends and family. Using photocopies makes sharing photos inexpensive, and the copier can be used to enlarge or reduce the photos to size. The copied photos can be cropped, glued, and manipulated like any paper image.

If possible, use a color copier to copy black and white photos — you'll get much better results. You can also ask the operator to adjust the copier so the copies will look like antique sepia-toned prints.

Beautiful Baby

Open size: 7-1/4" x 11"

Folded size: 7-1/4" x 5-1/2"

Techniques: 📷

Supplies

Paper:
Card stock, light pink, 8-1/2" x 11"
Printed paper with pink lace design,
    7-1/4" x 6-1/2"
Laser-cut lacy paper
Color copy of photo, 4-1/4" x 5-3/4"

Decorative Elements:
Gel pen, white

Tools & Other Supplies:
Glue stick

Step-by-Step

1. Fold the pink card stock to 7-1/4" x 5-1/2".
2. Fold one long edge of the printed pink lace paper 1" to cover the front of the card and wrap to the back. Attach to card front with glue.
3. Glue the photo to the center front of the card.
4. Trim paper lace motifs. Apply glue-stick adhesive to the backs. Affix corners to card front, overlapping photo. See project photo for placement.
5. Use a gel pen to make white dots around the edge of the photo for trim. ❑

Vacation Photo Frame

The frame can be easily removed from the card. Its magnetic strips will hold it to a fridge or filing cabinet. Be sure to point this out in the message so the recipient understands this is a card and a gift in one!

Open size: 8" x 12"

Folded size: 8" x 6"

Techniques:

Supplies

Paper:

Two-tone card stock, turquoise/white, 8" x 12"

Heavy textured paper, purple, 7-1/2" x 5-1/2"

Wavy corrugated paper, tan, 4" x 6"

Wavy corrugated paper, black

Card stock, 4" x 6"

Photo, 3-1/2" x 5"

Decorative Elements:

24 gauge wire - turquoise, blue

18 gauge wire - magenta

5 assorted buttons

Acrylic metallic paints - teal, pink

Tools & Other Supplies:

Magnet strips, self-adhesive

Foam brush

Needle tool

Round-nose pliers

Needlenose pliers

Wire cutters

Glue stick

Double-sided adhesive

Step-by-Step

1. Cut a 2-1/2" x 4-1/2" opening in the center of the tan corrugated paper to make the frame. Tape the photo in place at the back.
2. Use the foam brush to paint just the ridges of the black corrugated paper with acrylic paint. Let dry. Cut into assorted triangles.
3. Arrange the triangles and buttons as desired around the frame. With the needle tool, poke holes through the triangles and frame for the wire trim. Use the round-nose pliers to shape the wire and insert ends through the holes. Tape at back of frame.
4. Use more lengths of wire to attach the buttons to the frame. Keep some of the wire tails to the front. Twist them into decorative spirals.
5. Cover the back of the frame with a piece of card stock. Secure with double-sided adhesive.
6. Attach the self-adhesive magnet strips to the back of the frame. Check bond and reinforce if necessary.
7. Center the frame on the textured purple paper. Poke holes through the purple paper at the upper left and lower right corners of the frame. Using 24 ga. wire, attach the frame to the purple paper at opposite corners so the frame can be easily removed from the card.
8. Score and fold the turquoise/white card stock in half with turquoise facing out. Center the frame assembly on the outside front panel of the card and affix with double-sided adhesive. ❏

Sisters

Open size: 10-1/2" wide x 5-1/4" tall

Folded size: 5-1/4" square

Techniques: 📷

Supplies

Paper:

Purchased card and envelope, off-white

Two identical color copies of photo that fit card front

Decorative Elements: Metallic pen, gold

Tools & Other Supplies:

Dimensional adhesive dots

Micro-tip scissors; Glue stick

Step-by-Step

1. Trim one copy of the photo and glue to front of card.

2. Use the gold pen to draw a border around the photo. (I make it a little askew for an interesting look.)

3. Trim figures from second copy of the photo.

4. Position dimensional adhesive dots to the figures in copy of the photo attached to the card.

5. Position the cutout figures over their counterparts. ❏

Rustic Sepia

Open size: 13" x 6"

Folded size: 6-1/2" x 6"

Techniques: 📷 ❏

Supplies

Card stock - white, 2 pieces each 6-1/2" x 6", 1 piece 5-1/2" x 4-1/2" on which to attach photo

Patterned background paper - tan and ecru print, 6-1/2" x 6"

Handmade embossed floral paper with torn edges, 5" x 6"

Color copied photo, 3-1/2" x 4-1/2"

Decorative Elements:

Raffia; 3 self-adhesive photo corners

Tools & Other Supplies:

Paper edgers, deckle pattern

Small-holed paper punch; Double-sided adhesive; Glue stick

Step-by-Step

1. Trim small white card stock piece with deckle edgers to be 1/4" larger than the photo on all sides. This edging recalls snapshots from the 40s and 50s. Glue the photo to the white rectangle.

2. Glue the patterned background paper to one of the large white card stock pieces.

3. Attach the photo to the patterned panel, using three photo corners. (The top left corner will extend under the handmade paper when the card is finished.)

4. Fold the handmade paper the long way, with about 1-1/2" to the back and the rest to the front, to create a spine for the card.

5. Attach the remaining piece of white card stock to the inside of the spine.

6. Punch three sets of holes into the front part of the spine. Weave raffia in and out of the holes through both layers.

7. Use double-sided adhesive to attach the card front to the inside surface of the spine front. ❏

Birthday Cards

What could be more personal for someone's special day than a handmade card? This section contains three cards; one is just right for young children.

Left to right: Vintage Year, Nothing Fishy

Vintage Year

Pictured on page 69

This is a flat card – the message pulls out from the little pocket glued to the front of the card. The grape stickers are mirror images (the same image facing left and right, with exactly the same die cut), so I could make front and back images on the pullout card-in-a-card.

Overall size: 4-1/2" x 5-3/4"

Techniques:

Supplies

Paper:
Card stock, white, 4-1/2" x 5-3/4" for base card

Two-tone card stock, lilac/light lilac, 6-3/8" x 3-1/4" for message piece and 3" x 3-1/4" for pocket

Decorative Elements:
Embossing stencil with grapes motif

Stencil with birthday phrases, "Celebrate" and "Happy Birthday"

Punches - spiral, floral border

Artists' pastels (chalk) - green, purple

Ink dauber, metallic lavender

Stickers, grapes

Tools & Other Supplies:
Cotton swabs

Corner shaper scissors

Micro-tip scissors

Glue stick

Glue pen

Double-sided adhesive

Step-by-Step

Base Card:

1. Stencil-emboss grape bunches along the right side of the white card.

2. Tint embossing with soft color by lightly rubbing with a cotton swab that has been swiped over artist pastels.

Pocket:

1. Score 1/4" flaps on the bottom and sides of the pocket. Fold toward back, with dark paper color facing out.

2. Score and fold a 3/4" flap at the top and cut away corners so this flap can be folded forward. Miter the corners of the narrow flaps so they will lay flat behind the pocket.

3. Punch floral border on the front flap. Use corner shaper scissors to round off the corners.

4. Punch spirals in the body of the pocket. Turn one over to reveal the other color. Glue to pocket.

Card Pattern
(actual size)

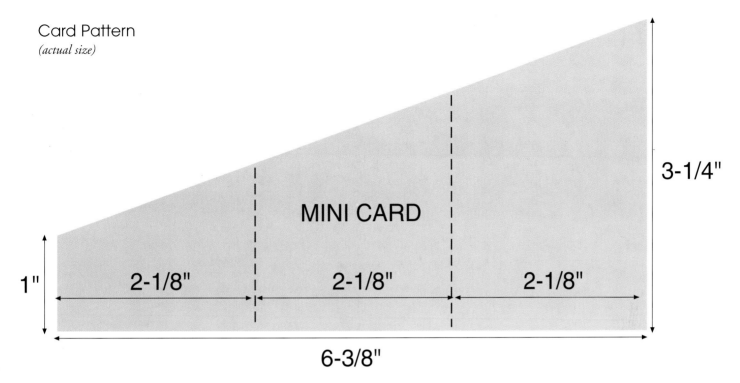

Mini Card:

1. With lilac side facing out, cut and score the remaining piece of two-tone paper according to the pattern. Fold into three panels.

2. Open flat and stencil-emboss a birthday message across all three panels.

3. Apply a grape sticker extending from the top of each panel.

4. Turn the card over and apply a mirror-image sticker to the back of each grape sticker, being careful to align them precisely.

Assembly:

1. Place the pocket on the white card and lightly mark the position of the sides.

2. Use ink dauber with Happy Birthday stencil to apply the message along the left side and bottom of the card.

3. Apply narrow strips of double-sided adhesive to the side and bottom pocket flaps and attach to the white card.

4. Fold the mini-card and insert it in the pocket. ❑

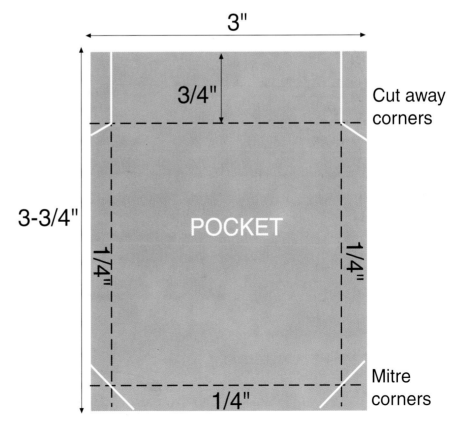

Nothing Fishy

Pictured on page 69

The checkerboard image on this card is created by cutting an image from wrapping paper into strips and weaving strips of tissue.

Open size: 11-3/4" x 7"

Folded size: 8" x 7"

Techniques: ❏

Supplies

Paper:

Card stock, bubbles design,
   12" x 7" for base card

Handmade paper, aqua, 7" x 5"

Handmade paper, blue, 7" x 3-1/2"

Framed fish image from wrapping paper,
   6" x 6"

Pearlescent tissue paper, blue, 6" x 6"

Self-adhesive metallic foil, magenta,
   3-1/2" square

Hologram film, green, 3-1/2" square

Decorative Elements:

Glitter paint or glue - purple, teal

Marking pen, purple

Tools & Other Supplies:

Cellophane tape

Double-sided adhesive

Glue stick

Step-by-Step

1. Score 4" from bottom of bubble paper and fold up flap, right sides together.

2. Coat back of aqua paper with glue stick and adhere to white side of bottom flap.

3. Tear edge of blue paper, coat with glue, and adhere to bottom flap, leaving about 1" of aqua paper exposed.

4. Tear edge of layered handmade and bubble paper panel.

5. Apply double-sided adhesive to the back of the hologram film. Cut the number for the child's age, using one of the patterns provided, from both the metallic foil and the hologram film.

6. Apply the foil number to the aqua and blue layered flap. Attach the hologram number on top of metallic number using double-sided adhesive and placing it slightly offset.

7. Write "you're" with purple glitter paint. Dot around the number with teal glitter paint. Set aside to dry.

Weaving:

8. Starting next to frame, cut vertical slits 1/4" apart all across the fish image. Cut through the bottom frame, but end the cuts at the top where the frame meets the fish image.

9. Cut the blue tissue into 1/4" strips. Weave the tissue strips horizontally into the fish image, ending just above the bottom of the frame.

10. Tape at back to hold the tissue strips in place and re-align the bottom frame.

Assembly

11. Attach the woven fish image to the top of the bubble paper panel.

12. With flap of card opened, write a message below the fish panel ("There's nothing fishy about this wish – Happy Birthday") with a purple marking pen. ❑

Young at Heart

Open size: 8-1/2" x 11"

Folded size: 8-1/2" x 5-1/2"

Techniques: ○

Supplies

Paper:

Card stock, sage green with flecks, 11" x 8-1/2" for base card

Handmade paper, cream with gold marbling, 8" x 5-1/2" for torn motif

Card stock, pale mint green, 3" x 4" for top card layer

Decoupage paper, antique birthday motif, 2-3/4" x 1-3/4"

Vellum paper, 2" x 6-1/2" for message ribbon

Purchased vellum envelope, 6" x 9"

Decorative Elements:

Sheer ribbon, light spring green, 1-1/4" wide, 16" long

Brass embossing stencil, ribbon border motif

Gilding paste, gold

Rubber stamp with message ("The Heart that Loves Is Always Young")

Embossing ink

Embossing powder, gold

12 green iridescent seed beads

Small charm, gold rose

Fabric paint, iridescent

Metallic paint pen, gold

Tools & Other Supplies:

Paper edger, pinking design

Paper embosser, wave design

Micro-tip scissors

Glue stick

Glue pen

Double-sided adhesive

Jeweler's glue

Step-by-Step

1. Glue the antique birthday motif to the mint card.

2. Stencil-emboss ribbon borders to frame the birthday motif on mint card.

3. Use a metallic paint pen to outline the edge of the birthday motif.

4. Glue seed beads to the top and bottom outer corners, using photo as a guide for placement.

5. Run the strip of vellum through the wave embosser.

6. Stamp and emboss the message with gold embossing powder on the bottom end of the vellum strip. Trim both ends with pinking edger.

7. Score and fold the green card stock in half.

8. Tear the edges of the marbled cream paper to roughly 5" x 8". Center and attach to front of folded green card stock.

9. Fold the sheer ribbon in half. Notch the ends with scissors.

10. Arrange and glue the layers in place: sheer ribbon, vellum strip, and embossed green panel.

11. Glue the gold charm in place with jeweler's glue. ❏

Wedding Cards

A one-of-a-kind greeting card is a perfect way to show a couple how special they are, and making a card allows you to create a personal message for special people. Ribbons and lace are appropriate trimmings.

Pictured top to bottom: Together Forever, Congratulations, Bridal Shower

Together Forever

Pictured on page 77

Visit the bridal section of a craft store to find the inexpensive wedding bands used to adorn the front of this card.

Open size: 6-1/2" x 10"

Folded size: 6-1/2" x 5"

Techniques: ❏ ♥

Supplies

Paper:

Card stock, light blue, 6-1/2" x 10", scored and folded to 5" x 6-1/2" for base card

Vellum - two pieces 6-1/2" x 2", and one piece 6" x 9" for message insert

Flowered paper from wallpaper or wrapping paper, 5" x 6-1/2"

Laser-cut paper trellis

Photo of house front from magazine

Decorative Elements:

Sheer ribbon, blue, 1/2" wide, 24" long

2 wedding bands

Alphabet stencil with 3/4" tall letters

Tools & Other Supplies:

Paper edgers

Stylus

Micro-tip scissors

Glue stick

Glue pen

Double-sided adhesive

Step-by-Step

1. Trim the magazine image to fit behind the paper trellis. Attach to the trellis with glue pen or glue stick.

2. Cut a slit in the lower front of the flowered paper piece, following lines in the design, that the trellis bottom can slip in.

3. Place the trellis in the slit and attach to the flowered paper with glue stick or pen.

4. Score 2" wide vellum piece 1/2" from the left long edge. Stencil-emboss "FOREVER" on the 1-1/2" wide panel.

5. Score the other piece of vellum 1-1/2" from the left long edge. Stencil-emboss "TOGETHER" on the larger side of panel.

6. Glue the 1/2" flaps of the embossed vellum pieces to the back of the flowered paper so that the embossed part of vellum folds over onto front of flowered paper.

7. Glue this floral piece to the front of the blue card.

8. Open the vellum flaps on the card front. Carefully cut 1/2" slits 1/8" from the edge for the ribbon to pass through. Re-fold.

9. Thread the ribbon through the slits so the ends are to the outside front. Knot. Slide the rings together and attach them to the ribbon with a pretty bow. Trim the ribbon ends with inverted V-cuts.

10. Fold and crease the 6" x 9" vellum piece to measure 6" x 4-1/2". Insert this piece into blue card. Leave this piece loose, or glue at fold to blue card.

11. On the vellum insert, write your message using a gold gel pen. The message in this card reads, "May you walk life's path hand in hand." ❏

Congratulations

Pictured on page 77

This card opens by lifting the lacy vellum flap to reveal a message. It is suitable for an engagement or wedding. The message inside was printed on 8-1/2" x 11" purple-dot vellum using a computer and laser printer before being trimmed to 4-1/2" x 7-1/4".

Open size: 6-1/2" x 16-1/4"

Folded size: 6" x 9"

Techniques:

Supplies

Paper:
Velveteen paper, purple, 6" x 9" for bottom layer of card
Card stock, purple, 6" x 9", for back of card
Stardust paper, lilac, 5-1/2" x 8-1/4"
Vellum, printed with overall lace design, 6" x 8" for front flat
Vellum, lavender dots, 8-1/2" x 11", message piece
Vellum, plain, 3-1/2"
Romantic image from magazine or wrapping paper, 3-3/4" x 6"

Decorative Elements:
Foam stamp, lacy heart motif, about 3-1/2" across
Embossing ink
Embossing powder, pearl white
Fabric paint, white pearl
Seed beads, white pearlescent
Paper punch, 1/8" heart
Paper punch, 1/2" heart
Paper punch, floral border
Paper edger, Victorian design

Tools & Other Supplies:
Computer and laser printer
Needle tool
Micro-tip scissors
Glue stick
Glue pen
Double-sided adhesive

Step-by-Step

1. Print out your message on lavender-dot vellum, using a computer and laser printer. Trim paper to 4-1/2" x 7-1/4".
2. Stamp the lacy heart image on plain vellum 3-1/2" square. Emboss with pearlescent powder. Carefully cut out this heart, including the openings within it.
3. Glue heart to the bottom of the lacy vellum paper, centering the heart from side to side, with point at bottom edge of vellum piece.
4. Use paper edgers to remove 1-1/2" at the bottom edge of the lacy vellum at each side of heart, leaving the lower part of the heart motif extending beyond the trimmed edge.
5. Punch tiny hearts along the edged vellum. Paper-prick around the hearts and along the edge.
6. Score and fold a 1/2" flap at the top of the vellum panel.
7. Place dots of fabric glue on the heart applique and set seed beads into the glue. Set aside to dry thoroughly.
8. Punch heart and border motifs along the bottom edge of the stardust panel. Paper-prick around the punched design.
9. Center the stardust panel on the velveteen panel and attach with double-sided adhesive.
10. Position the romantic image on the stardust panel and attach.
11. Use small dots of double-sided adhesive to attach the top edge of the lavender dotted vellum panel with message to the top edge of the stardust panel.
12. Attach the appliqued lacy vellum panel to the top of the card, gluing the flap to the back.
13. To reinforce the card, glue the purple card stock panel to the back. ❑

Bridal Shower

Pictured on page 77

Open size: 6-1/2" x 7"

Folded size: 4" x 5"

Techniques:

Supplies

Paper:

Printed paper with soft lace motif, 8-1/2" x 11" plus a second sheet for the envelope

Printed paper with blue lace motif, 8-1/2" x 11"

Decorative Elements:

Fabric Lace, at least 1" wide, 5" long

Stickers with romantic images - one with a bride and one with a hand
Option: Decoupage images

Stencil with 1/2" letters

Stamp pad, blue

Fine-tip markers - magenta, purple

Small length of fine chain

Small jump ring

Tiny gold heart charm

Metallic paint pen, gold (for envelope)

Tools & Other Supplies:

Decorative corner scissors

Micro-tip scissors

Small sponge dauber

Needlenose pliers

Glue stick

Glue pen

Double-sided adhesive

Step-by-Step

Card:

1. Lightly mark a 4" x 5" rectangle on the soft lace printed paper. (This will be the card back.)

2. Attach a sticker to the left side of the card, outside of the pencil mark, but touching the pencil mark. Attach another sticker, upside down, at the bottom of the card, outside the pencil mark, but touching the pencil mark. *Option:* Use decoupage images and glue in place.

3. Attach lace, using double-sided adhesive, along the opposite edge of the card, to the wrong side of the paper.

4. Using a glue-stick, wrong sides together, attach blue lace paper to the soft lace paper.

5. From the back side, trim the rectangle and cut out around the stickers. See photo.

6. Fold the sticker flaps toward the front of the card.

7. Stencil the message on the part of the card that is not covered by the flaps as shown on the photo.

8. Open the card. Handwrite additional messages with fine-tip pens. Place them so they won't show when the card is folded.

9. Size the fine chain to fit the wrist of the hand motif. Join the ends and add the charm with a jump ring.

Envelope:

1. Make an envelope with a decorative flap, using the pattern provided.

2. Edge the flap with a metallic gold paint pen. ❑

Envelope Pattern

Enlarge @125% for actual size or use measurements provided.

Start with
8-1/2" x 11" sheet.

Cut along
solid lines.

Score and fold along dashed lines.
Cut slight angles
along dotted lines.
Glue back panel
to side flaps.

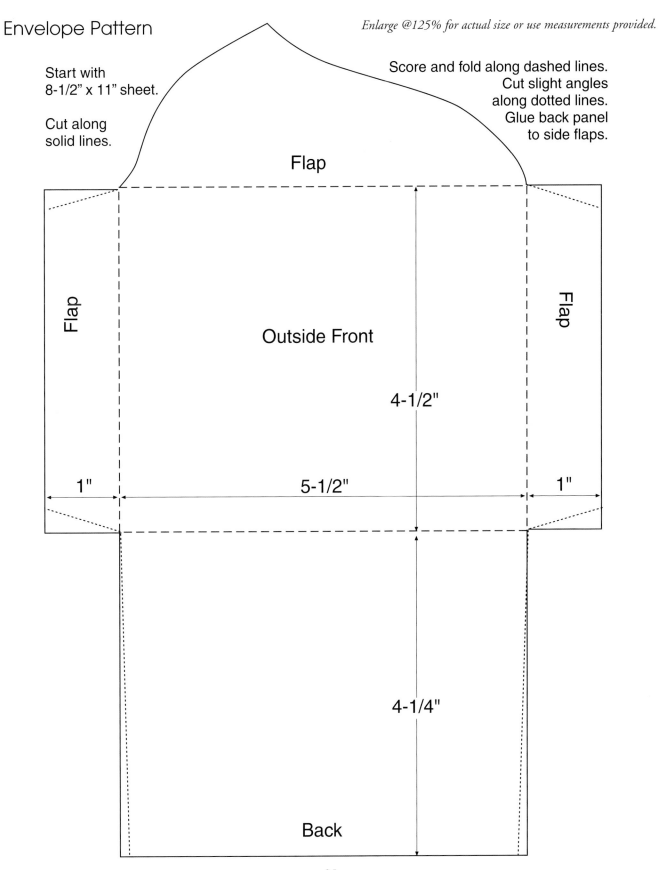

Flap

Flap

Flap

Outside Front

4-1/2"

1"

5-1/2"

1"

4-1/4"

Back

New Baby Cards

New parents will treasure a keepsake handmade card for a new baby. A handmade card is a wonderful way to express your congratulations or invite guests to a baby shower. Make them in pretty pastels — pink and blue, of course, plus lavender and soft yellows and greens.

Pictured at right top to bottom: Baby Shower, Folded Diaper Card, Baby Name

may your life be

showered

Tuesday's child is full of grace

Monday's child is fair of face

Wednesday's child is full of woe

BABY SHOWER!
for Millicent Smith
Saturday, July 14
2 pm
at Sarah Jones'
2858 West Oaktree Ave.

Thursday's child has far to go

Friday's child is loving and giving

Saturday's child works hard for a living

IS FOR HAPPY BABY

H

IS FOR HAPPY BABY

Folded Diaper Card

Pictured on page 83

This card folds to look like a diaper, so it makes a perfect card for congratulating or announcing a birth. It's also a good shape for a baby shower card, as shown. Hold it together with a diaper pin-shaped sticker. For mailing, purchase or make envelopes that meet postal requirements (3-1/2" x 5" minimum in the United States). You can also use the diaper pattern to make envelopes for gift enclosures. To make multiples of this card, set up the lettering for the card and the vellum panels on plain white paper and take to a copy shop. Put vellum and card stock in the copying machine and run off as many copies as you need (plus a few extras, to take care of any mistakes you might make during finishing).

Open size: 8-1/2" x 11"

Folded size: 4" x 4"

Techniques:

Supplies

Paper:
Card stock, white with printed lavender hearts, 8-1/2" x 11"
Vellum, pink gingham, 3-1/2" x 9-1/2"
Card stock, small pieces of pink and blue

Decorative Elements:
Rubber stamps with banner and baby images
Stamp pads, purple ink and blue ink
Colored pencils, blue and purple
Marking pen, blue
Embossing ink pen
Embossing powder, purple

Tools & Other Supplies:
Embossing heat tool
Glue pen
Double-sided adhesive
Micro-tip scissors

Step-by-Step

1. Copy the pattern provided on page 85 to the printed card stock at a copy center or hand-write it yourself.
2. Cut out, score, and fold the card stock as indicated in Fig. 1.
3. Stamp baby images on pink and blue paper with purple ink.
4. Cut the stamped diaper from the blue paper and attach it to a baby stamped onto pink paper using a glue pen. Stamp baby buggy and color with pencils.
5. Cut out buggy and babies using a micro-tip scissors.
6. Stamp banner onto blue paper with blue ink. Write a message on the banner with blue marking pen. Cut out banner.
7. Cut and fold vellum panel as indicated in Fig. 2.
8. Handwrite your message on the vellum panel, using the embossing ink pen, and apply purple embossing powder.
9. Use a glue pen to apply adhesive to the backs of the stamped images and attach to vellum.
10. Position double-sided adhesive to the back of the vellum, behind the banner image, and attach to center panel of card, matching folds.

Shower Invitation

1. Make the card the same way as instructed previously.
2. Set up the message for your invitation to fit within a 3-1/2" square area and repeat up to six times on an 8-1/2" x 11" sheet of plain white paper. You can handwrite it, print it out on a computer, or use the template provided on page 89.
3. Make multiple copies of the message on blue checked vellum. Cut out.
4. Use stickers to hold the vellum panel to the card stock and to embellish the invitation. ❏

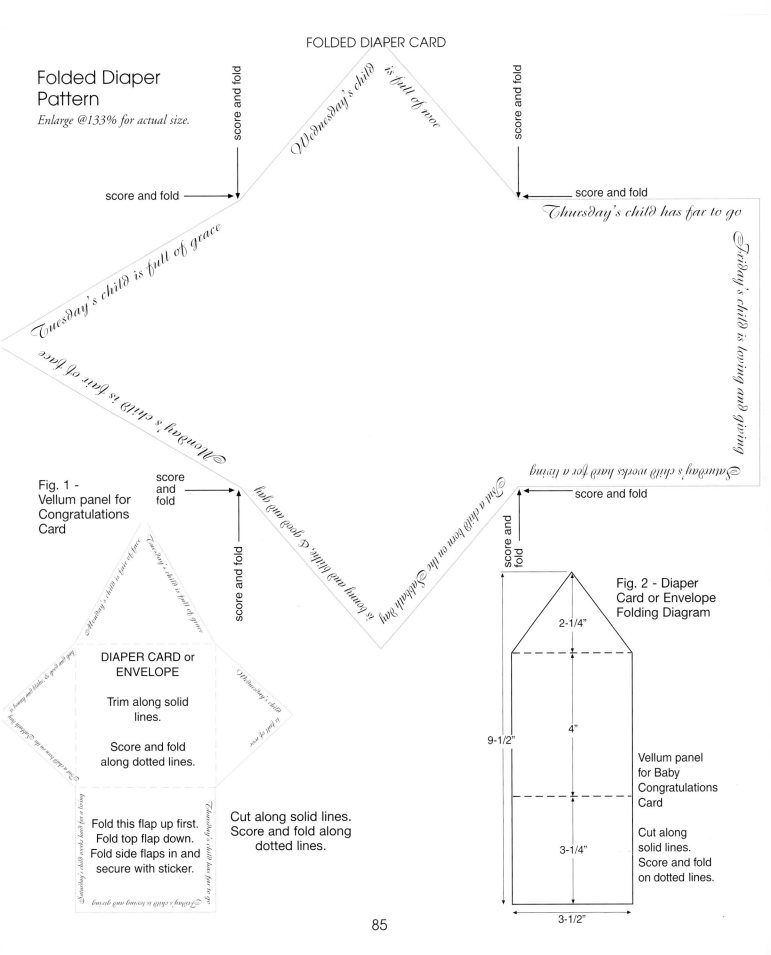

Folded Diaper Pattern

Enlarge @133% for actual size.

score and fold

score and fold

Wednesday's child is full of woe

score and fold →

Thursday's child has far to go

Tuesday's child is full of grace

Friday's child is loving and giving

Monday's child is fair of face

Fig. 1 - Vellum panel for Congratulations Card

score and fold →

score and fold

Saturday's child works hard for a living

← score and fold

score and fold

But a child born on the Sabbath Day

is bonny and blithe, & good and gay

DIAPER CARD or ENVELOPE

Trim along solid lines.

Score and fold along dotted lines.

Fold this flap up first. Fold top flap down. Fold side flaps in and secure with sticker.

Cut along solid lines. Score and fold along dotted lines.

Fig. 2 - Diaper Card or Envelope Folding Diagram

2-1/4"

4"

9-1/2"

3-1/4"

3-1/2"

Vellum panel for Baby Congratulations Card

Cut along solid lines. Score and fold on dotted lines.

score and fold

Baby Name

Pictured on page 83

The gingham-patterned vellum envelope for this card folds to look like a diaper. Hold it together with a pin-shaped sticker. To mail the finished card in its diaper envelope, purchase or make a mailing envelope that meets postal requirements (3-1/2" x 5" is the U.S. minimum).

Open size: 11-3/4" wide x 12" tall

Folded size: 3-1/2" x 3-1/2"

Techniques:

Supplies

Paper:

Card stock, pink, 11-3/4" x 12-1/2"

Tissue, blue, 11-3/4" x 12-1/2"

Vellum, blue dots, 6-1/2" x 3-1/2"

Vellum, lavender gingham, 8-1/2" x 11" (for envelope)

Printed paper, pink and blue background

Pictures of babies in sizes indicated on pattern

Decorative Elements:

Stickers with baby themes

Circle templates, 2-1/2" and 2-1/8"

Oval template, 4" x 2-1/2"

Stencil, letter "H"

Embossing ink

Embossing powder, purple

Tools & Other Supplies:

Paper edgers, pinking, scallop

Marking pens - purple (fine tip), magenta, blue

Embossing heat tool

Spray adhesive

Glue stick

Step-by-Step

Card:

1. To make the white side of the pink card stock blue, spray with adhesive and attach blue tissue paper.

2. Cut out, score, and fold the card, following the pattern.

3. Trim the bottom edge of the front with scallop edgers.

4. Using the scallop edgers, cut a blue strip from blue tissue and glue to card front.

5. Apply a stork sticker to the front. Where the sticker extends off the paper, back with vellum and trim to sticker shape.

6. Stencil and emboss a purple "H" on the pink and blue printed paper.

7. Use a circle template to draw a 2-1/8" circle around the letter with fine-tip purple marker. Write "IS FOR HAPPY BABY" inside the circle.

8. Draw a 2-1/2" circle around the first circle. Trim with pinking edgers to make a "seal."

9. Score and fold the blue dot vellum in half. Trim with scallop edger 1/4" shorter than card front.

10. Attach the seal to the vellum with glue stick. Apply a narrow band of adhesive from the glue stick to the back of the card, near the fold, and attach the vellum overlay to the card.

11. Use the oval template to draw a shape on the pink and blue printed paper. Cut oval with scalloped edgers.

12. With fine-tip purple marker, write message inside the oval shape.

13. With card open, glue a baby image to panels A and B. Glue the oval shape to panels B and C. Glue baby images to panels C through G.

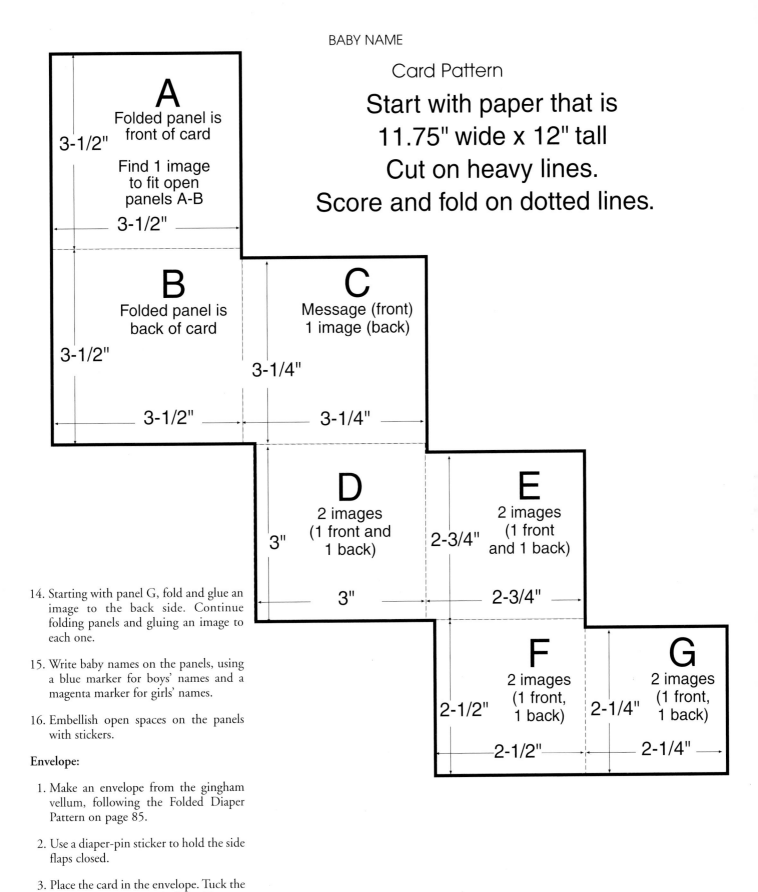

Card Pattern

Start with paper that is 11.75" wide x 12" tall Cut on heavy lines. Score and fold on dotted lines.

A
Folded panel is front of card

Find 1 image to fit open panels A-B

3-1/2"
3-1/2"

B
Folded panel is back of card

3-1/2"
3-1/2"

C
Message (front)
1 image (back)

3-1/4"
3-1/4"

D
2 images
(1 front and 1 back)

3"
3"

E
2 images
(1 front and 1 back)

2-3/4"
2-3/4"

F
2 images
(1 front, 1 back)

2-1/2"
2-1/2"

G
2 images
(1 front, 1 back)

2-1/4"
2-1/4"

14. Starting with panel G, fold and glue an image to the back side. Continue folding panels and gluing an image to each one.

15. Write baby names on the panels, using a blue marker for boys' names and a magenta marker for girls' names.

16. Embellish open spaces on the panels with stickers.

Envelope:

1. Make an envelope from the gingham vellum, following the Folded Diaper Pattern on page 85.

2. Use a diaper-pin sticker to hold the side flaps closed.

3. Place the card in the envelope. Tuck the top flap behind the side flaps. ❏

Baby Shower

Pictured on page 83

Card stock that measures 12" x 12" can be found in the scrapbooking department. Flower stamens are a craft material used in the creation of artificial flowers.

Open size: 4-1/2" x 13-1/2"

Folded size: 4-1/2" x 6-3/4"

Techniques: ○ ▢

Supplies

Paper:

Card stock, cloud design, 4-1/2" x 12"

Card stock, blue and white checks, 4-1/2" x 5-1/2" for inside of cover

Vellum, blue dots, 4-1/2" x 6-3/4"

Umbrella image from wrapping paper

Decorative Elements:

Stickers with baby and heart motifs

Rub-on lettering

6 flower stamens, pink

9 seed beads, baby blue

Foil-wrapped cord, blue, 3"

Tools & Other Supplies:

Foam carpet tape, self-adhesive

Micro-tip scissors

Glue stick

Double-sided adhesive

Jeweler's glue

Step-by-Step

1. With the right side facing you, score the cloud paper 5-1/4" from the bottom edge. When folded, your card will have a front panel that is shorter than the back, and the clouds will be oriented correctly on the front.
2. Cut out the umbrella image, omitting the handle. Glue to the card front along the lower edge. Trim around the umbrella shape.
3. Position the blue checked paper on the inside of the card front and trace around the umbrella shape. Trim to match outside front. Do not attach to card yet.
4. Apply the rub-on lettering ("may your life be showered") to the front of the card above the umbrella.
5. Cut apart the flower stamens in the middle. Slide a seed bead on each half.
6. Use jeweler's glue to attach a stamen and bead to the wrong side of the umbrella motif at the end of each umbrella rib.
7. Glue three beads to the end of the foil-wrapped cord. Glue the other end of the cord to the wrong side of the umbrella to make a handle. The handle should not extend beyond the bottom edge of the folded card.
8. Affix the blue checked paper to the back of the card front, using a glue stick.
9. Attach a baby buggy sticker to the inside of the card back.
10. Apply rub-on lettering ("with infantile delight!") to the vellum panel.
11. Use small dots of double-sided adhesive at the top to attach the vellum panel to the inside of the card back. (The lower portion of this will show when the card is folded.)
12. Attach a baby rattle sticker to the vellum in the upper left corner.
13. Apply a heart sticker to plain paper. Cut out close to the image. Place a small piece of foam carpet tape to the back of the heart to raise it off the paper slightly. Stick the heart to the vellum panel. ❑

At right: **Invitation Template**
Photocopy this page onto any color paper and create your own invitation for a baby shower.

Baby Shower!

For:

When:

Where:

Baby Shower!

For:

When:

Where:

Baby Shower!

For:

When:

Where:

Baby Shower!

For:

When:

Where:

Baby Shower!

For:

When:

Where:

Baby Shower!

For:

When:

Where:

Special Days Cards

Create a special card to mark a special day. This section includes cards for Father's Day, Mother's Day, Graduations, Anniversaries, Thanksgiving, Valentine's Day, and Easter.

Pictured clockwise, from top left: Father's Day, Thanksgiving, Happy Anniversary, Graduation Day

Father's Day

Pictured on page 91

This handsome tri-fold card is easily made.

Open size: 6-3/4" x 11-3/4"

Folded size: 8-1/2" x 5-1/2"

Techniques: ⊞ 🔖

Supplies

Paper:

Card stock, green, 8-1/2" x 11" for base card

Marbled paper, green, 8-1/2" x 4-1/4" for front left panel

Handmade textured paper, copper, 8-1/2" x 4" and 3" x 3" for front right flap

Heavy duty aluminum foil

Decorative Elements:

Foam or rubber stamps with leaf motifs, to fit within 2-1/4" squares

Acrylic paint, any color

Rubber stamp with message ("Happy Father's Day")

Embossing ink

Silver embossing powder

Tools & Other Supplies:

Pinking paper edgers

Stylus

Brayer or credit card

Embossing heat tool

Spray adhesive

Glue stick

Double-sided adhesive

Step-by-Step

Foil Embossing:

1. Fold a piece of aluminum foil in half, shiny sides together, to yield a double layer at least 4" x 9". Open the foil and spray with adhesive, then fold back together and smooth with a brayer or the edge of a credit card.

2. Mark three 2" squares on one side of the foil with a stylus, leaving at least 1/2" between the squares. (The side of the foil you work on will be the back of your finished motifs.)

3. Use acrylic paint to stamp a leaf image on the wrong side of each square with a foam stamp. Let dry.

4. Still working on the back of the foil, trace around each leaf image with the stylus to emboss. TIP: if the stylus catches on the foil, rub the stylus on some wax paper to make it glide smoothly.

5. Add veins to the leaves with the stylus. Create a background around each leaf with free-form squiggles, lines, and cross-hatches, using the stylus on the wrong side of the foil.

6. Trim the squares with pinking edgers approximately 1/8" from the embossed borders. The sides of these squares without the paint will be the front side.

Card:

1. Score and fold the green card stock 4-1/4" and 9-3/4" from one end to create a card with two flaps.

2. To the wide (left) flap, attach marbled paper with glue stick or double-sided adhesive.

3. Score and fold the textured copper paper 2-1/2" from one long edge. Tear the other long edge. Apply glue stick adhesive to the entire back side of the copper paper.

4. Align the straight long edge with the fold of the right flap and adhere. Fold the copper paper together, creating an extended flap on the right side of the card. When glue has dried, tear the folded edge of the copper paper.

5. Stamp and emboss the father's day message on a 3" square of textured copper paper, using silver embossing powder.

6. Trim the embossed piece with pinking edgers to fit on the narrow flap of the card. Attach to card with glue stick.

7. Fold the copper flap to overlap the marbled flap. Center the foil-embossed images in a vertical row. Attach foil pieces to card front with double-sided adhesive. ❏

Thanksgiving

Pictured on page 91

Open size: 8-1/2" x 11"

Folded size: 8-1/2" x 5-1/2"

Techniques: ▢

Supplies

Paper:

High gloss card stock, white, 8-1/2" x 11"

Printed paper for liner, leaf design,
    8-1/2" x 11"

Vellum paper, white with overall leaf print
    in white, 5" x 8"

Velveteen paper, sage green
    (2-1/4" x 2-1/2" scored and folded
    to 1-1/2" x 2-1/2")

Decoupage motif, leaves

Decorative Elements:

Stickers, leaves

Rubber stamp with message
    ("Happy Thanksgiving")

Rubber stamps with assorted leaf images

Variegated metal leaf, copper and gold

Dry adhesive in the shape of leaves

Marking pens, assorted colors

Metallic paint pen, copper

Tools & Other Supplies:

Micro-tip scissors

Glue stick

Double-sided adhesive

Step-by-Step

1. Score high gloss paper and fold 2-3/4" from
   each short end.
2. Open up and rubber-stamp leaf images all over the flaps, overlapping and
   bleeding the images past the edges.
3. Shade each leaf stamp with marking pens. Test color combinations on scrap paper.
   Re-ink the stamp and apply to the card.
4. Use the tip of the bone folder to transfer the dry adhesive leaf shapes, rubbing firmly
   to release the glue from the carrier sheet.
5. Apply the variegated metal leaf to the adhesive and brush away excess.
6. Use the copper paint pen to paint the edges the flaps where they meet in the middle
   of the card. Protect the inside of the card with scrap paper if you do this with the flaps
   folded.
7. Score and fold the printed leaf paper to match the card. Adhere to inside of card with
   adhesive along the top edge only.
8. Stamp the greeting on the vellum panel, using orange and brown marking pens to ink
   the stamp.
9. Use leaf-shaped stickers to hold the vellum panel in place inside the card.
10. Apply two 3/4" strips of adhesive to the widest part of the back of the velveteen paper.
    Remove the liner of one adhesive strip and secure the velveteen flap in place. Remove
    the remaining liner and attach the velveteen panel to the left flap of the card front,
    centered vertically.
11. Carefully cut out the decoupage leaves image and glue to velveteen panel. ❑

Graduation Day

Pictured on page 91

Open size: 8-1/2" x 11"

Folded size: 8-1/2" x 5-1/2"

Techniques: ◯ ▦

Supplies

Paper:

Wrapping paper with butterfly motifs, 5-1/2" x 8-1/2"

Vellum paper, 8-1/2" x 11" plus a 4" square piece

Printed paper with cloud design, 6" x 8-1/2"

Decorative Elements:

Sheer ribbon, 1/2" wide, 36" long

Metallic paint pen, gold

Butterfly images cut from additional wrapping paper

Rubber stamp ("Congratulations Graduate")

Rubber stamp (wings)

Embossing ink pad

Embossing powders - silver, clear, purple pearlescent

Flocking powder, purple

Marker, blue

7 seed beads, purple

Large seed bead, purple

Flower stamen, black

Miniature butterfly net

Fabric paint, purple with glitter

Gel pen with black ink

Tools & Other Supplies:

Circle cutter

Micro-tip scissors

Glue stick

Double-sided adhesive

Jeweler's glue

Step-by-Step

1. Score the vellum sheet and fold in half.
2. Score a 1/2" flap along the left edge of the cloud paper. With double-sided adhesive, attach the butterfly paper to the cloud paper so the butterflies face out and the cloud paper makes the inside right panel of the card.
3. With the circle cutter, make a 2" window in the vellum card front. Gild the edges of the circle with the gold metallic paint pen.
4. Align the inner card (with butterflies showing through) with the vellum and cut a matching circle in the butterfly paper.
5. Using a black gel pen, write a message on the vellum card front ("Never stop chasing your dreams..."). Working quickly, before the ink dries, emboss with clear powder.
6. On a separate piece of vellum, stamp four wing shapes. Emboss with purple pearlescent powder.
7. Color the back sides of the wings with a blue marker. Cut out wings, adding a small tab at the base of each, and set aside.
8. Draw a butterfly body on the paper surface of double-sided adhesive and cut out.
9. Apply body to a small piece of vellum. Remove the second paper liner and sprinkle flocking powder on the adhesive. Tap off excess.
10. Cut the body out of the vellum, leaving a 1/16" margin all around. Cut small slits for inserting the tabs of the wings.
11. Slip wing tabs in slits and adhere each wing with a small dab of jeweler's glue on the underside of the body. Let dry.
12. Carefully bend each wing up slightly to stand away from the body. Fold the flower stamen in half and glue to the back of the butterfly's head to make antennae. Glue the butterfly assembly to the front of the card with jeweler's glue. Let dry.
13. Make a row of small fabric paint dots along the butterfly's back. Place a seed bead on each wet dot, using the large bead for the head. Set aside to dry.
14. Stamp a graduation message on the inside of the card and emboss with silver. Position the message so it won't show through the circle window.
15. Use glue stick to adhere a butterfly motif cut from wrapping paper to the inside of the card so it shows through the window. Add another butterfly to the inside, using photo as a guide for placement.
16. With jeweler's glue, affix the miniature butterfly net so part of it shows through the window.
17. Assemble the inner and outer card components. Hold together with small bead of adhesive from a glue stick along the fold toward the back. Tie the ribbon around the card and finish with a bow on the outside front. ❑

Happy Anniversary

Pictured on page 91

*Three handmade papers – tan, blue, and white –
and a decoupage motif adorn this plain white card.*

Open size: 8-1/2" x 5-1/2"

Folded size: 4-1/4" x 5-1/2"

Techniques:

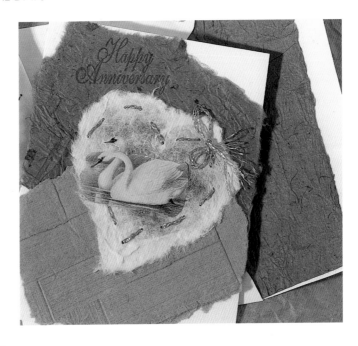

Supplies

Paper:

Purchased blank card and envelope, white

Handmade textured papers - white, blue, tan

Swans motif from decoupage paper

Decorative Elements:

Decorative gold thread or cord

Rubber stamp ("Happy Anniversary")

Blue ink stamp pad

Large-eye embroidery or darning needle

Tools & Other Supplies:

Glue stick

Step-by-Step

1. Tear the blue and tan papers and arrange for background, using photo as a guide. Apply glue where they overlap to hold them together.

2. Tear the white handmade paper into a heart shape. Glue it to the background.

3. Use the needle and thread to stitch a decorative running stitch to border the edge of the heart with gold thread or cord. Tie in a bow at top right.

4. Stamp "Happy Anniversary" on the blue paper.

5. Glue the swan motif on the heart.

6. Glue the entire assembly to the front of the card.

7. Tear away any of the background paper that extends beyond the edges of the card.

8. Line the envelope with blue paper. ❏

Easter Greeting

Open size: 5-1/4" x 10-1/4"

Folded size: 5-1/4" x 5-1/4"

Techniques: ○ ◻ ♟

Supplies

Paper:

Purchased blank card and envelope, white

Stardust paper - magenta, chartreuse, yellow, pink with magenta dots, lavender with purple stripes

Decorative Elements:

Rubber stamp ("Happy Easter")

Stamp pad, rainbow colors

Punch, spiral design

Stickers of Easter eggs

Seed beads, pink

Fabric paint, purple glitter

Tools & Other Supplies:

Paper edgers - wave design, pinking

Pencil

Stylus

Double-sided adhesive

Glue pen

Step-by-Step

1. Mark 1/2" along right edge of card front on the inside.
2. Using double-sided adhesive, attach pink dotted stardust paper to the left half of the card front and lavender striped stardust paper to the right half, butting the two at the center.
3. With the wave edger, trim away 1/2" on the right front edge, using your pencil line as a guide.
4. Use the flower pattern to outline this simple shape on the paper liner of double-sided adhesive. Trim loosely around the stem and leaves.

5. Apply stem-and-leaves adhesive shapes to the back of chartreuse stardust paper and the flower shape to the back of yellow stardust paper.
6. Cut out the flower, stem, and leaves. Stick these to front of card, covering the seam between the patterned stardust papers with the stem.
7. Stick an egg-shaped sticker on each flower petal.
8. Cut a strip of magenta stardust paper 5-1/4" x 1-1/2". Trim one long edge with wave edger. Attach magenta paper to the inside of the card along the right edge, letting the wavy edge extend slightly beyond the straight edge of the card. Use glue pen to adhere.
9. Stamp the Easter message on the inside of the card and envelope flap with rainbow ink. Add an egg sticker above the greeting on the inside.
10. Punch spirals from the chartreuse and yellow stardust papers. Use the glue pen to apply adhesive to the back of each spiral. Glue them along the edge of the inside border.
11. Glue a chartreuse spiral to the center of the flower blossom on the card front.
12. Apply small dots of fabric paint around the flower center. Place a seed bead in each dot of paint. Set aside to dry. ❑

Pictured above: open cards, Easter Greetings and Valentine's Day. *Pictured at right:* Valentine's Day, Easter Greeting

Flower Pattern

Enlarge @155% for actual size.

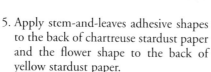

I Love You!

Happy Easter

Valentine's Day

Pictured on page 96 (opened) and 97

This card carries a heart-shaped pin that can be removed and worn on the recipient's lapel.

Open size: 8" x 11"

Folded size: 8" x 5-1/2"

Techniques: ○ ▢ ✳ ♟

Supplies

Paper:

Embossed hearts and spirals card stock, purple, 8" x 11"

Embossed hearts card stock, off-white, 4" x 7"

Card stock with printed with hearts and dots design, purple on white, 8-1/2" x 8" for liner

Small scrap of card stock for pin back

Stardust paper, gold, 2" x 8"

Velveteen paper, deep red, 6" x 6"

Textured handmade paper, purple, 5" x 5"

Decorative Elements:

Instant gold gilding foil and adhesive (the adhesive is printed in the shape of the letters and border elements)

Open-mesh ribbon, red, 2" wide, 20" long

Seed beads, purple

Fabric paint, purple glitter

Punch, spiral motif

Stamp, heart design (for liner)

Stamp pads, gold, purple

Marker, purple

Pin back jewelry finding

Assorted seed and bugle beads, golds and reds

Heart charm, gold

Tools & Other Supplies:

Beading thread and needle

Paper edgers, wide scallop design

Low-temp glue gun and glue

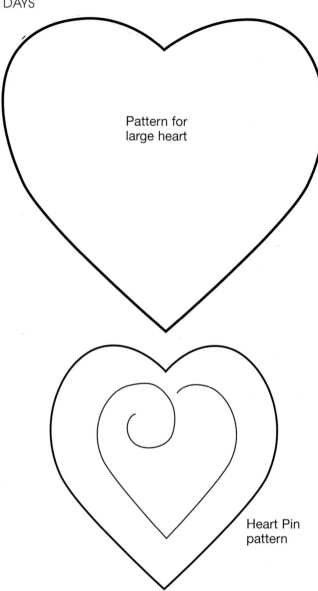

Pattern for large heart

Heart Pin pattern

Step-By-Step

Outside of Card:

1. Score and fold the embossed purple paper in half, with purple to outside.

2. Attach strip of gold stardust to right edge of inside.

3. Trim right edge through both layers with wide scallop edger. Trim left edge 1/4" narrower.

4. Punch spirals along the left edge so the gold stardust shows through.

5. Center and attach off-white embossed panel to the front of the card.

6. Wrap the mesh ribbon around and attach with glue on inside of card.

7. Tear the textured purple paper and the red velveteen paper into heart shapes, using pattern provided.

8. Rub the gold stamp pad across the purple textured heart to highlight.

9. On the purple heart, place random dots of fabric paint. Set a seed bead into each dot of paint. Set aside to dry.

10. Use instant gilding foil and adhesive to decorate the velveteen heart.

Liner:

1. Score and fold heart-printed card stock 4-1/4" from right edge.

2. Stamp a purple heart on the right panel. Add a message with purple marker.

3. Attach the liner to card with double-sided adhesive at the left edge of the opened card, with folds aligned.

Heart Pin:

1. Using the pattern provided, with a low-temp glue gun draw a bead of glue in the shape of a small heart on red velveteen paper. Let the glue cool for a few minutes, until it becomes cloudy or opaque.

2. Press the gilding foil on the glue, being sure to make contact on sides as well as top of the glue bead.

3. Tear around the heart shape, leaving a 1/8" margin.

4. Using the beading thread and needle, string and stitch several strands of beads in the small heart near the bottom. Add the heart charm to the end of the longest strand. Knot all the strands at the back of the paper heart and secure with jeweler's glue.

5. Cut a small heart from card stock and affix to back of pin with double-sided adhesive.

6. Glue the pin finding to the pin back near the top.

Assembly:

1. Overlap and glue the larger heart shapes in place as shown in the photo.

2. Attach the heart pin by its finding to the open-mesh ribbon near the top of the card. ❑

Lacy Mother's Day

Pictured on page 101

Open size: 8" x 12"

Folded size: 8" x 6"

Techniques:

Supplies

Paper:
Card stock - gold with flecks, 11" x 7-1/2", scored and folded to 5-1/2" x 7-1/2"
Velveteen paper, burgundy, 4-3/4" x 6-1/2"
Card stock, cream, 4" x 5"
Scrap paper for mask
Small cut paper silhouette of cupid
Paper doily, 8" x 12"

Decorative Elements:
Sheer ribbon, 1" wide, 36" long
Stencils for paper-pricking and stencil-embossing
Rubber stamp, background leaf motif
Embossing ink
Embossing powders, pearlized, gold

Tools & Other Supplies:
Dimensional adhesive dot

Embossing heat tool
1/4" hole punch
Paper crimper
Needle tool
Stylus
Double-sided adhesive

Step-by-Step

1. Score and crease gold flecked card stock. Folded size will be 5-1/2" x 7-1/2". Fold doily in half. Insert card stock into doily and punch two holes in the fold, 1" from both top and bottom edges. Insert ribbon and tie into a bow on outside.

2. Most cut silhouettes are made of black paper. To change one to metallic gold, lay the silhouette on a piece of scrap paper and blot the surface with embossing ink, using the pad as an applicator. Sprinkle gold embossing powder over the silhouette and emboss with heat tool.

3. Prepare the cream panel by cutting a mask for the stamping. (I used the central portion of the paper-pricking stencil for the shape.) The opening in the mask includes the area to be stamp-embossed, with enough paper surrounding the opening to cover the rest of the cream stock. With the mask in place, stamp a design with embossing ink. Remove the mask and sprinkle pearlized powder over the ink. Use heat tool to emboss.

4. Paper-prick and stencil-emboss border designs on the cream panel.

5. Roll the velveteen paper through the crimper.

6. Center the cream panel on the velveteen panel and adhere with double-sided adhesive.

7. Affix the velveteen panel with the cream panel attached to the front of the doily using double-sided adhesive.

8. Attach the gold silhouette to the center of the card front with a dimensional adhesive dot. ❑

Mother's Day Heart

Open size: 6-3/4" x 13-3/4"

Folded size: 6-3/4" x 5-1/2"

Techniques: ❑

Supplies

Paper:

Printed overall pattern card stock - cream on one side, patterned with peach background on other, 8-1/2" x 6-3/4"

Printed overall pattern card stock - cream on one side, patterned with olive background on other, 5-1/4" x 6-3/4"

Card stock, cream, 10-3/4" x 6-3/4"

Sheer checked paper, 4" x 4"

Printed paper photo frame, heart motif

Clip art image of woman's head and neck copied on light pink paper

Decorative Elements:

Marking pens with ink in coordinating colors

Colored pencils

Tools & Other Supplies:

Micro-tip scissors

Glue stick

Double-sided adhesive

Step-by-Step

1. Score and fold cream card stock 5-1/4" from one edge to create the front panel of the card.

2. Use colored pencils to softly tint the eyelids, cheeks, and lips of the clip art image. Trim image to fit the inside panel of the card. Attach with glue stick.

3. Cut away center of heart frame. Lay the frame on the clip art image to determine a good position. Close the card and flip it over so the wrong side of the frame is to the inside of the card. Keeping it in that position, trace the frame opening on the inside front panel of the card. Carefully cut out with a craft knife.

4. Align the olive patterned paper on the outside card front. Trace the frame opening on the back. Cut out.

5. Use a glue stick to adhere the sheer checked square of paper over the opening of the card front.

6. Align and attach the olive patterned panel to the card front with double-sided adhesive.

7. Glue the heart frame in place on the olive paper.

8. Use the marking pens to write a message to your mother on the inside of the card.

9. Score the peach patterned paper 5-1/2" from one end. Trim the edge of the 3" flap to follow the pattern printed on the paper.

10. Affix the 5-1/2" panel to the outside back of the card. Fold the 3" flap around the front of the card, overlapping the heart frame. ❑

Pictured at right, left to right: Lacy Mother's Day, Mother's Day Heart

Christmas Cards

The Christmas holidays are a time when families gather and we take the time to keep in touch with far-flung friends. A handmade card is a thoughtful way to remember friends who display Christmas cards as a part of their holiday decor. In this section, you'll find a variety of holiday designs.

Pictured, clockwise from top left: Poinsettia Greeting, Noel in Silver & Gold, Joy in Beads, Copper Simplicity, Family Photo Foldout

Joy in Beads

Pictured on pages 103 and 108 (opened)

Open size: 10" x 5-1/2"

Folded size: 5" x 5-1/2"

Techniques: ○ ▢

Supplies

Paper:

Stardust card stock, burgundy,
    10" x 5-1/2"

Stardust card stock, white, 5" x 5-1/2"
    plus scraps

Velveteen paper, burgundy, 4-1/4" x 5"

Vellum, printed with gold stars,
    4-3/4" x 9-1/2"

Decorative Elements:

26 gauge wire, 20" plus more for
    attaching

Seed beads - silver, white, red

Punches - spiral, star

Glitter paint or glue, iridescent

Metallic paint pen, gold

Paper silhouette, child with doll

Tools & Other Supplies:

Paper edgers, deckle style

Needle tool

Round-nose or needlenose pliers

Double-sided adhesive

Pass wire back through beads at this area

Loop wire around itself at intersection

Punch tiny holes in paper and wire beaded word to card

Punch tiny holes in paper and wire beaded word to card

Loop wire around itself at intersection

Step-by-Step

1. Twist a small loop in one end of the wire and string on the seed beads – mostly silver ones, but occasionally a white or a red one. As you go, follow the pattern for the word "Joy" and bend the beaded wire into the shape of the letters. Twist the wire over itself once when you reach an intersection; double back through at the top of the "o" and outer top of "y." At the end of the "y," twist a small loop to hold the beads in place, Trim excess wire.

2. Position the beaded wire word against the velveteen panel. Punch small holes with the needle tool in the paper as indicated on the pattern. Bring up additional wire from the back of the paper, around the beaded wire, then through the second hole. Twist the attaching wire tightly to the back of the paper.

3. Center and attach the velveteen panel to the white stardust panel.

4. Punch spirals and stars from additional white stardust paper and attach to decorated panel. Embellish with dots of glitter paint or glue.

5. Score the back (blank) side of the burgundy stardust sheet at the center mark and very lightly across the front side in the same place, using a craft knife and a very light touch. Carefully fold the paper, stardust to inside.

6. Outline all four edges of the vellum panel with a metallic gold paint pen. Let dry.

7. Carefully trim all four edges with a deckle paper edger. Score and fold sheet in half.

8. Hand write a message on the bottom half of the gold star vellum with a gold paint pen.

9. Paint the paper silhouette with gold paint pen and attach to upper half of vellum sheet.

10. Glue two small red beads on the silhouette and let dry.

11. Apply double-sided adhesive to back side of vellum, hiding it behind the silhouette applique. Attach the vellum to the stardust background.

12. Attach the decorated card front to the appropriate blank side of the burgundy stardust sheet. ❑

Family Photo Foldout

Pictured on 103 and 108 (open)

Open size: 9-3/4" x 14-3/4"

Folded size: 5" x 6"

Techniques: 📷 ♥

Supplies

Paper:

Two-tone paper, red/green, 12" x 18" sheet

Vellum, green checks. 5" x 5"

Vellum - red dots, 4" x 4-1/2" and
    9-1/2" x 4-1/2"

Vellum, green, 3" x 4"

Photocopies of family photos, assorted

Decorative Elements:

Punches - star, floral border

Glitter glue - gold, red

Metallic paint pen, gold

Stencil, Christmas tree

Gel pens - gold, black

Tools & Other Supplies:

Paper edgers, Victorian design

Compass

Stylus

Double-sided adhesive

Glue stick

Step-by-Step

1. Follow the pattern provided, cut and fold the red/green paper, with the green side on the front cover. Trim the circular panels with the edgers.

2. Gild the edges, front and back, with the metallic paint pen.

3. Cut a 1-1/4" x 5" strip of the red/green paper. Punch floral border motifs along one edge with a star in the middle. Trim the strip with edgers to a sloping triangular shape and overlap 1/2" on the green card front at the bottom edge. Glue in place.

4. Gild the edges of the green-checked vellum panel and the

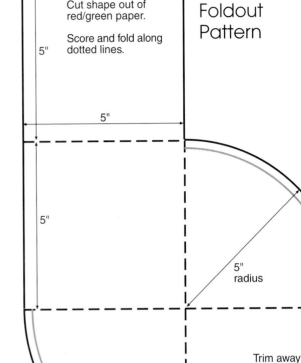

Photo Foldout Pattern

Cut shape out of red/green paper.

Score and fold along dotted lines.

5"

5"

5"

5" radius

Trim away 1/4" of circle with decorative edgers.

smaller red-dot vellum panel. Score and fold a 1/2" flap at the top edge of each. Center and affix first the green-check vellum, then the red-dot vellum to the front of the card, gluing the flaps to the back.

5. Stencil-emboss the Christmas tree on the green vellum. Trim close to edges and glue to card front.

6. Embellish tree with tiny dots of gold and red glitter glue.

7. Score and fold the remaining red-dot vellum panel in half. Add photos and messages with black gel pen. Attach to inside front of card with double-sided adhesive, hidden behind a photo.

8. Attach remaining photos to all circular red panels, taking care to avoid having photos cross the folds.

9. Fold up the bottom half of the red circle. Add photos to the green panels. Fold the green panels together. Add more photos to the last green quarter-circle panel.

10. Write messages on the green and red photo panels with the gold gel pen. ❏

Noel in Silver & Gold

Pictured on page 103 and 109 (opened)

Open size: 5-1/2" x 11"   Folded size: 5-1/2" x 5-1/2"

Techniques:

Supplies

Paper:
Vellum card stock, 5-1/2" x 11"
Vellum paper, 4" square
Vellum, silver
Vellum, silver checks, 8-1/2" x 11" (for envelope)
Stardust paper, red
Stardust patterned papers - silver stripes, silver dots, silver
   diamonds, gold stripes, gold dots, gold stars

Decorative Elements:
Stencil with embellished letters to spell NOEL
Sticker, silver lacy heart
Metallic paint pen, gold
Gel pen, gold
Metallic colored pencils - silver, gold
Lightweight gold cord, 12"

Tools & Other Supplies:
Paper edger, Victorian style
Punch, 1/8" heart
Needle tool
Double-sided adhesive
Glue pen
Stylus

Step-by-Step

Card:
1. Score vellum card stock 2-3/4" from each end. Fold flaps toward center.
2. Mark four 2" squares on silver vellum. Stencil-emboss one letter ("NOEL") on each square. Cut out.
3. With a metallic gold paint pen, outline a 4-3/4" x 2-3/8" rectangle on each flap of the card, then divide each rectangle into squares to create a gold frame for each embossed letter.
4. Attach the embossed letters to the flaps, using the glue pen.
5. Prick the gold background around the letters with a needle tool.
6. Open the flaps. Cut four 2" squares of patterned stardust paper. Attach to the inside of the vellum to hide the adhesive.
7. Cut heart with flaps from red stardust paper, using pattern provided. Carefully score the flaps with a craft knife on the right side of the paper. Close flaps.
8. Cut flap shapes from silver and gold patterned stardust papers. Glue to white sides of heart flaps.
9. With needle tool, punch a hole in each flap. Attach a 6" length of thread through each hole. Knot to hold in place.
10. Cut vellum paper heart, using pattern provided. Trim with edgers.

11. Paper-prick vellum heart and punch 1/8" hearts around edge.
12. Attach silver heart sticker in center of vellum heart.
13. Write message around the sticker with silver metallic pencil ("close to our hearts.")
14. Use double-sided adhesive to attach the heart with flaps to the inside of the card.
15. Write around the heart ("Let us keep Christmas") with gold gel pen.
16. Tie the heart flaps closed with looped bow.
17. Since it will show through the envelope, draw a heart over the adhesive area on back of the card. Color with metallic silver and gold colored pencils.

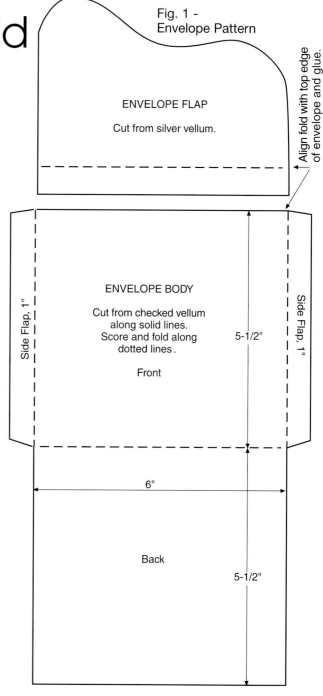

Fig. 1 - Envelope Pattern

Align fold with top edge of envelope and glue.

ENVELOPE FLAP
Cut from silver vellum.

Side Flap, 1"

Side Flap, 1"

ENVELOPE BODY
Cut from checked vellum along solid lines.
Score and fold along dotted lines.

Front

5-1/2"

6"

Back

5-1/2"

Patterns

Enlarge @117% for actual size.

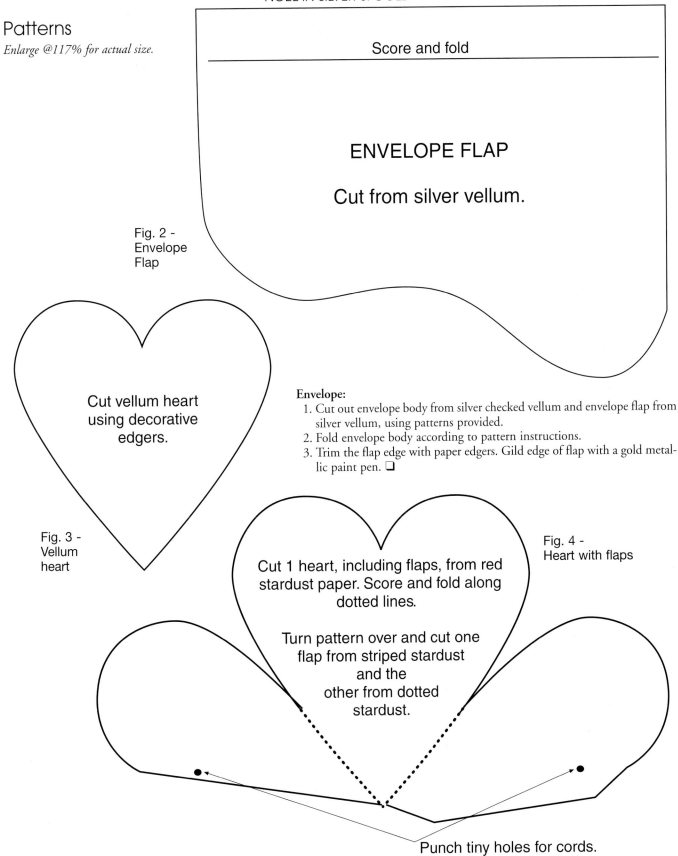

Score and fold

ENVELOPE FLAP

Cut from silver vellum.

Fig. 2 -
Envelope
Flap

Cut vellum heart
using decorative
edgers.

Envelope:
1. Cut out envelope body from silver checked vellum and envelope flap from silver vellum, using patterns provided.
2. Fold envelope body according to pattern instructions.
3. Trim the flap edge with paper edgers. Gild edge of flap with a gold metallic paint pen. ❏

Fig. 3 -
Vellum
heart

Fig. 4 -
Heart with flaps

Cut 1 heart, including flaps, from red stardust paper. Score and fold along dotted lines.

Turn pattern over and cut one flap from striped stardust and the other from dotted stardust.

Punch tiny holes for cords.

Copper Simplicity

Pictured on 103 and 109 (opened)

Open size: 8-1/2" x 11"

Folded size: 8-1/2" x 5-1/2"

Techniques: ✳

Supplies

Paper:

Handmade paper, newsprint overlaid with crinkled kraft-colored tissue, 6" x 11"

Printed card stock, gold ginkgo-leaf design, 8-1/2" x 11"

Vellum, card weight paper, 7-1/2" x 10"

Decorative Elements:

Acrylic paint, pthalo green

Composition leaf, copper (2-3/4" x 4")

Brass embossing stencil, border design

Rubber stamp with ginkgo leaves

Stamp pad, brass

Metallic paint pen, copper

Gel pen, gold

Tools & Other Supplies:

Corner shaper scissors

1" paint brush

Double-sided adhesive

Step-by-Step

1. Score and fold a 1/2" flap at one long edge of the handmade paper. Have the copper leaf rectangle within easy reach.

2. Apply paint loosely to the center of the handmade paper, using photo as a guide. While the paint is still wet, slide the leaf in place. Pat lightly with a clean brush to adhere. Set aside to dry.

3. Stencil-emboss borders on the vellum.

4. Trim the corners of the vellum with corner shaper scissors. Score and fold in half.

5. Stamp ginkgo leaf design on the upper half of the vellum.

6. Hand write a greeting on the left side of the vellum sheet.

7. Score and fold the gold ginkgo paper in half. Attach the vellum sheet inside with small dots of double-sided adhesive.

8. Attach the decorated handmade paper to the front of the card.

9. Write a message around the gold-leaf rectangle with gold gel pen. ❑

Pictured left to right, opened: Joy in Beads, Family Photo Foldout. See instructions on pages 104 and 105.

Poinsettia Greeting

Pictured left to right: Noel in Silver & Gold, Copper Simplicity, Poinsettia Greeting

Open size: 13-1/4" x 6"   Folded size: 8-1/2" x 6"

Techniques: ✳ ⊞ ❐ ♟ ♥

Supplies

Paper:
Card stock, burgundy, 8-1/2" x 6"
Velveteen paper, sage green, 5-1/4" x 6"
  plus scraps
Velveteen paper, burgundy, 5-1/2" x 4-1/2"
Velveteen paper, red, 4-1/2" x 4-1/2"
Paper, cream, 8-1/2" x 11"
Vellum paper, 2" square
Purchased vellum envelope, 6" x 9"

Decorative Elements:
Stencil with poinsettia motif
Colored pencils - burgundy, ochre, green
Gold foil lettering kit
Rubber stamp, all-over leaf design
Rubber stamp, pocket watch
Embossing powders - clear, gold
Embossing ink

Tools & Other Supplies:
Paper edgers, Victorian design
Low-temp glue gun
Double-sided adhesive
Glue pen
Computer with laser printer

Step-by-Step

1. Stamp an all-over leaf design as a background on burgundy paper. Emboss with clear powder. Trim along bottom edge of burgundy paper with paper edgers.
2. Use foil lettering kit to apply "Merry Christmas" along bottom edge of green velveteen paper. Trim edge with edgers.
3. Print out holiday message using computer and laser printer on cream paper. Trim to 4-1/2" x 9". Score and fold so message appears on bottom half.
4. Stamp and emboss the watch on vellum. Trim close to edges. Color the back of the watch face with ochre colored pencil. Glue to top half of cream sheet with glue pen.
5. Score a 1/2" flap across one end of burgundy velveteen paper. Trim bottom with edgers.
6. Trace poinsettia stencil on red velveteen with burgundy colored pencil. Go over lines on red velveteen with low-temp glue gun. Add small dots in center. Let cool. Apply foil to cover the raised glue lines. Cut around the shape, leaving the petals intact to form a solid flower.
7. Trace poinsettia leaves on sage velveteen with green pencil. With green pencil, draw veins in the leaves on the sage paper. Cut out each leaf.
8. Attach poinsettia and leaves to the burgundy velveteen panel.
9. Attach the flap at the top to the back of the sage velveteen panel. Attach both to the embossed burgundy card, aligning the tops.
10. Attach the top of the folded cream panel to the back side of the burgundy velveteen. ❑

Metric Conversion Chart

Inches to Millimeters and Centimeters

Inches	MM	CM
1/8	3	.3
1/4	6	.6
3/8	10	1.0
1/2	13	1.3
5/8	16	1.6
3/4	19	1.9
7/8	22	2.2
1	25	2.5
1-1/4	32	3.2
1-1/2	38	3.8
1-3/4	44	4.4
2	51	5.1
3	76	7.6
4	102	10.2
5	127	12.7
6	152	15.2
7	178	17.8
8	203	20.3
9	229	22.9
10	254	25.4
11	279	27.9
12	305	30.5

Yards to Meters

Yards	Meters
1/8	.11
1/4	.23
3/8	.34
1/2	.46
5/8	.57
3/4	.69
7/8	.80
1	.91
2	1.83
3	2.74
4	3.66
5	4.57
6	5.49
7	6.40
8	7.32
9	8.23
10	9.14

Index

Index